D0598047

CALGARY PUBLIC LIBRARY

APR   2018

make your own
SOAPS
LOTIONS
MOISTURIZERS

0 11557 01539 3

The original German edition was published as *Kosmetikwerkstatt*.

Copyright © 2013 frechverlag GmbH, Stuttgart, Germany (www.frech.de)

This edition is published by arrangement with Claudia Böhme Rights & Literary Agency, Hanover, Germany (www.agency-boehme.com)

This edition copyright © 2015 by Stackpole Books

Published by
STACKPOLE BOOKS
5067 Ritter Road
Mechanicsburg, PA 17055
www.stackpolebooks.com

All rights reserved, including the right to reproduce this book or portions thereof in any form or by any means, electronic or mechanical, including recording or by any information storage and retrieval system, without permission in writing from the publisher. All inquiries should be addressed to Stackpole Books, 5067 Ritter Road, Mechanicsburg, PA 17055.

While author and publisher have made every effort to ensure that ingredient specifications and working notes in this book have been carefully checked, no guarantees can be given. Any liability by author and publisher for possible errors or damages must be excluded. This publication with all of its parts and the recipes contained within are protected by copyright. Reproduction and distribution of the contents of this book other than for personal, noncommercial purposes, are prohibited and will be prosecuted under civil and criminal law. This applies especially to, but is not limited to, distribution of materials from this book through photocopies, broadcasting in film, radio and television, electronic media and the Internet as well as commercial usage of the presented recipes and techniques. If used for client consultation and teaching purposes, this book and its author have to be referenced.

Printed in the United States of America

10 9 8 7 6 5 4 3 2 1

First edition

PHOTOGRAPHS: frechverlag GmbH, 70499 Stuttgart, Germany; iStock and Shutterstock (pages 11–52); Jinaika Jakuszeit (step-by-step photographs); Lichtpunkt, Michael Ruder, Stuttgart (recipe photographs)
PRODUCT MANAGEMENT: Katrin Hartmann
EDITORS: Susanne Dubbers, Beeke Heller
LAYOUT: Karoline Steidinger and Tessa J. Sweigert
TRANSLATION: Katarina Sokiran
COVER DESIGN: Wendy A. Reynolds

Library of Congress Cataloging-in-Publication Data

Jakuszeit, Jinaika, author.
 [Kosmetikwerkstatt. English]
 Make your own soaps, lotions, and moisturizers : luxury beauty products you can create at home / Jinaika Jakuszeit. — First edition.
     pages cm
 "The original German edition was published as Kosmetikwerkstatt."
 Includes index.
 ISBN 978-0-8117-1539-3
 1. Toilet preparations. 2. Skin—Care and hygiene. 3. Beauty, Personal. I. Title.
 TP983 .J2713
 646.7'2—dc23
                              2015032595

make your own

SOAPS
LOTIONS &
MOISTURIZERS

Luxury Beauty Products You Can Create at Home

JINAIKA JAKUSZEIT

STACKPOLE
BOOKS

Contents

Dear Reader,

For me, making my own skin care products is one of the most rewarding hobbies imaginable, and I hope to be able to evoke the same enthusiasm in you which I felt when I first discovered this wonderful pastime.

Making your own skin care products enables you to match recipes exactly to your skin's specific needs by pinpointing the perfect formula and recreating it anytime on your own.

Discover the wide variety of ingredients available to the ambitious home cosmetology lab technician today: From aloe vera and avocado oil, cocoa butter, carnauba wax, healing chalk and silk powder to Dead Sea salt and vitamin C—endless possibilities to create a unique and individualized skin care product are waiting for you!

Immerse yourself in the world of homemade skin care, and be inspired by the many options this book has in store. Enjoy exploring!

Basic Knowledge

Making your own beauty products is very easy when you adhere to a few basic rules. Cosmetic products generally consist of aqueous (water) and lipid (fat) phases, surfactants (for cleansing products), extracts and other nourishing substances, fragrances, and perhaps preservatives. Their manufacture in itself is no magic science: Your kitchen, a few common household tools and appliances, such as an electric mixer and immersion blender, as well as a few pieces of basic equipment like beakers and spatulas, will get you started. Weighing, mixing, and simmering ingredients and a little experimentation will have you on your way to your own personal care line in no time! When presented in pretty tubes, jars, or flasks, your products will be beautiful to look at and make excellent gifts for dear friends or beloved relatives.

Our Skin

Covering an area of about 1.5 m² to 2 m² (16 to 21.5 sq ft), the skin is the largest organ of the human body and our interface to the environment and our fellow creatures. It enables us to feel heat and cold, touch and pain, proximity and distance, and protects us from harmful external influences, germs, foreign substances, superficial mechanical injuries, and fluid loss.

Our skin is made up of three main layers:

* the upper skin (epidermis) with its appendages (glands, hair, and nails)

* the true skin (corium or dermis)

* the subcutaneous tissue (hypodermis or subcutis)

Epidermis and dermis, the two outer layers of the skin, are often referred to by their combined term, cutis.

The epidermis consists of multiple layers of flat cells comprised mostly of nucleated horny cells called keratinocytes. They produce keratin, a horny substance creating a water-repellent protective barrier. The upper skin contains sensory and melanin-producing cells. It is 0.03 to 4 mm (0.001 to 0.16 inches) thick, with the thickest parts located at the palms and soles of the feet, the areas of the body most exposed to mechanical stress. The skin is constantly renewing. Over a span of 30 days, skin cells complete a full renewal cycle, from their formation to their migration through the skin's layers to the cells' death. The process of shedding dead cells on the skin surface is called "programmed cell death."

The dermis mainly consists of connective tissue fibers, giving the skin both tensile strength and the needed elasticity. The German word "lederhaut" (leathery skin) for the dermis originates from namely this layer of the animal skin being turned into leather when tanning hides. This skin layer transitions smoothly into the fat layer below it, the hypodermis, where fat cells are held together by fibrous tissue. In the younger body, the tissue stores water, giving the skin its plump, youthful appearance. With increasing age, the dermis loses both collagen and elastin, so the skin becomes thinner and less able to transfer moisture to the epidermis, resulting in wrinkle formation. The upper layer of the dermis, the papillary layer (stratum papillare), consists of loose connective tissue, embedding fat cells, and a thin arrangement of elastic collagen fibers. Small, nipple-like extensions (interdigitations) of the dermis into the epidermis, called dermal papillae (DP), contain blood vessels (capillaries) supplying the epidermis with nutrients. The ridges formed by the dermal papillae greatly increase the surface area between the dermis and epidermis, prevent the dermal and epidermal layers from separating from each other, and facilitate gripping. The impressions left by these friction ridges are our fingerprints, unique for each individual.

The lower layer of the dermis is called reticular dermis (stratum reticulare) and consists of dense, irregularly arranged connective tissue containing collagen and elastic fibers as well as blood vessels, fatty tissue, hair follicles, sebaceous glands, nerve endings, and sweat gland ducts.

The hypodermis, with its loose connective tissue, acts as an intermediary layer between the skin and the underlying layers such as the epimysium (sheath of connective tissue around the muscle) and the periosteum (membrane covering the outer surface of the bones). The hypodermis accomodates the lower sections of the hair follicle roots as well as thermoreceptors and mechanoreceptors called Ruffinian endings. The main task of the subcutaneous fatty tissue is to cushion the inner organs and to insulate the body.

What enters our body through the skin depends mainly on the condition of the skin microbiome (skin flora) and hydrophobic lipid envelope (acid mantle) on the surface of the skin. The acid mantle holds sebum (an oily matter waterproofing the skin), sweat, the skin's own moisture, corneous cells, and other waste products. Its normal pH value ranges from 5.5 to 6.5. Since the skin flora is directly dependent on the integrity of the acid mantle, viruses and other disease-causing organisms can penetrate the skin when the pH value of this protective layer has been disturbed. The resident bacteria on the skin's surface can thrive best in an environment with a slightly acidic pH.

Most skin care products work at an epidermal level, so we want to take a closer look at this skin layer. The epidermis can be divided into five layers (listed from the innermost to the outermost one):

* basal layer (stratum basale)

* prickle cell or spinous layer (stratum spinosum)

* granular layer (stratum granulosum)

* clear layer (stratum lucidum)

* horny layer (stratum corneum)

The basal layer (stratum basale), the deepest of the five layers, is mostly made up of basal keratinocyte cells which divide to form keratinocytes. With new daughter cells constantly being built in this skin layer, old cells are automatically moved toward the surface of the skin, initially ending up in the prickle cell layer (stratum spinosum).

This layer is composed of eight to ten rows of cells with prickly extensions which connect cells with each other. This framework of intracellular connections bridging individual cells provides stability to the upper skin. This prickly cell layer is also home to lamellar granules called keratinosomes, or Odland bodies, which are secretory organelles releasing lipids which later form the skin's own protective layer.

The granular layer (stratum granulosum) is composed of three to five rows of cells. This is where the skin's cornification process (keratinisation) starts, with keratinocytes increasingly flattening and losing their nuclei. Fats released from here into the intercellular space build the base from which the skin's barrier layer is formed in the stratum corneum.

The clear layer (stratum lucidum) is named for its translucent appearance under a microscope. It is made up of three to five layers of dead, flattened karatinocytes. The keratinocytes of the stratum lucidum do not feature distinct boundaries and are filled with eleidin, an intermediate form of keratin. The thickness of the lucidum is controlled by the rate of mitosis (division) of the epidermal cells. In addition, melanosomes determine the darkness of the stratum lucidum.

The horny layer (stratum corneum) is made up of 25 to 30 rows of flat cells entirely filled with the horny material keratin, the space between the corneocytes taken up with the barrier layer like mortar between bricks. This gives the skin layer the necessary strength and also protects against evaporation. Corneocytes are constantly shedded—a perpetual cycle of birth, life, and death.

KARN SAMANVORAWONG/SHUTTERSTOCK.COM

Different Skin Types

Before you set out to find out the best suitable skin care products for your individual needs, it is important to determine your skin type.

There are six basic skin types:

* dry skin
* oily skin
* combination skin
* sensitive skin
* aging skin
* normal skin

To which one of these categories your skin belongs depends on various factors: the degree of oil production, your individual metabolism, and how much moisture your skin is able to produce and retain.

Additional factors that can influence your complexion are:

* hormonal influences during puberty or pregnancy

* hereditary disposition

* illnesses

* nutrition and lifestyle

* cosmetics

* climate, atmospheric humidity, and exposure to the sun and UV rays

11

The most considerable differences can be noticed in the facial skin. Just like the rest of your body, the skin of your face is subject to natural changes throughout your life. After age 45, most people tend to have normal to dry skin, while younger individuals often suffer from enhanced tallow secretion and acne-prone skin. Because the sebaceous glands are not fully developed before puberty, tallow secretion greatly increases at this stage in life, continuing through age 25. After this age, sebaceous production decreases.

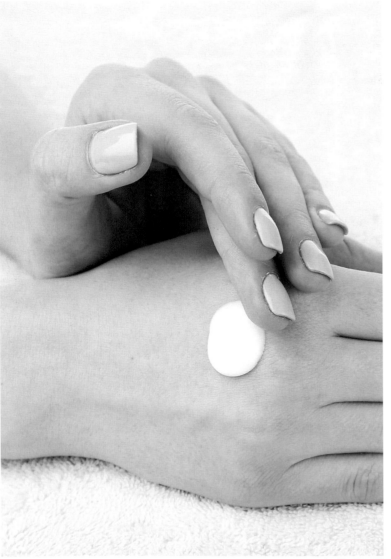

Dry Skin

The most common underlying cause for dry skin (sebostasis) is underactive sebaceous glands, resulting in inadequate lipid supply for the skin, which in turn causes dry, flaking, and reddened patches.

People who have dry skin rarely have to complain about impurities or large pores during adolescence. The more the skin matures, the more cosmetic care it will need because its own sebaceous glands produce less and less of the skin's own fat. Dry skin is also less elastic than other skin types. It becomes more easily damaged, allowing germs to enter and causing skin inflammation. People with dry skin are also more prone to increased wrinkling.

Among the causes for dry skin, besides natural disposition, are external factors such as stress and poor diet, as well as alcohol and tobacco consumption. Cold temperatures, overwashing, and low humidity, especially during the winter with central heating, can have a negative impact too.

Oily Skin (Seborrhoea)

This skin type is characterized by large-pored facial areas with overly oily and shiny chin and forehead caused by hyperactivity of the sebaceous glands, which are sensitive to fluctuating hormone levels and will react to inadequate nutrition. Women of this skin type may notice an increase in blackheads and pimples around the time of their menstrual periods, particularly in the T-zone, the area of the forehead, nose, and chin. The good news about oily skin is that in most cases, it is very robust and resistive to external influences.

Oily skin can be divided into two main types: Seborrhoea oleosa and seborrhoea dermatitis.

Seborrhoea Oleosa

Here, the mixing ratio between water and sebum creates a water-in-oil (W/O) emulsion (see pages 14–15), and the skin has a heightened water retention capacity, causing increased comedo formation and shiny facial skin with large pores.

Seborrhoeia Dermatitis

In this type, the mixing ratio is exactly reversed—to an oil-in-water (O/W) emulsion (see pages 14–15). The skin does not retain enough water, causing tightening and reddening of the skin upon contact with water. In seborrhoeic dermatitis, too, the skin has an excessive shine with pores appearing greatly enlarged.

AFRICA STUDIO/SHUTTERSTOCK.COM

Combination Skin

Combination skin, as its name implies, combines different skin types. In most cases, those are dry and normal skin or normal and oily skin. The oily areas of the face are mainly restricted to the T-zone (between forehead, nose, and mouth). The rest of the facial skin is either normal or dry.

Sensitive Skin

In this day and age, the vast majority of people suffer from this skin condition, often caused by intolerance of various ingredients prevalent in cosmetic products, such as fragrances, dyes, surfactants, or preservatives. Often the intolerance may be to just one ingredient, such as the type of oil used in a product, so people with sensitive skin have to test their tolerance to different cosmetics individually. For these people, I recommend using recipes with as few ingredients as possible, because this way, it is much easier to find out which one of the ingredients might be the culprit.

Aging Skin

Between ages 30 and 40, age-related skin changes due to reduced sebum production begin to be visibly noticeable. Generally, aging skin is mostly too dry, has a pale complexion, and has had its elasticity significantly reduced. Establishing a proper skin care regimen even before reaching this age is important to prevent the skin from drying out, causing unwelcome wrinkling, because once wrinkles have begun to emerge, the aid possible from topical creams will be limited. However, if the needs of one's skin are recognized at age 20 and a regular care and cleansing routine is started, the first signs of aging can be noticeably delayed.

Normal Skin

Normal skin has fine pores, an even surface, and is firm and smooth to the touch. Sebum production and skin moisture are in balance.

Exceedingly few people can enjoy such a skin type over the course of their whole life. If you belong to this lucky group, you can feel blessed. Use balanced skin care products containing not too much fat.

NATA-LIA/SHUTTERSTOCK.COM

Basics of Making Skin Care Products

What Is an Emulsion?

From a chemical point of view, many cosmetics are emulsions. In this book, too, most recipes will be based on emulsions. To ensure that later on there will always be the right "chemistry" between you and your very own homemade cosmetics, it is a good idea to acquaint yourself now with some basic knowledge about emulsions and how they work, so you will be able to draw on this knowledge when you try out recipes from this book or develop your own.

An emulsion is a very finely blended mixture of two normally nonmixable liquids, which in skin care might be jojoba oil and rose water. Because fatty substances and water naturally repel each other instead of

HOBITNJAK/SHUTTERSTOCK.COM

combining well, they have to be agitated to disperse one liquid into the other. An emulsifying agent will ensure that one of the two liquids forms droplets while the other encases them, creating a stable mixture. The outer phase (in which the droplets swim and the surfactant is more soluble) is called the continuous phase.

Skin care creams consist of three main components, so-called phases:

1. Lipid or fat phase (dispersed phase)—into this category fall butter, oils, waxes, stabilizers, coemulsifiers, and emulsifiers.

2. Aqueous or water phase (continuous phase)—this category includes water and hydrolates (see page 34) and, in a few instances, milk or fruit juice too.

3. Active agent phase—to this category belong, among other things, extracts, vitamins, gelling agents (thickening agents which ensure that the phases of an emulsion don't separate again), as well as essential oils. The active agent phase is an additional phase, giving cosmetics their scent, their characteristic consistency, and special efficacy.

There are two different types of emulsions:

* oil-in-water emulsion (O/W emulsion): Oil is the dispersed phase, water is the dispersion medium

* water-in-oil emulsion (W/O emulsion): Water is the dispersed phase, oil is the external phase

In an oil-in-water emulsion, oil droplets are encased by water. This type of emulsion feels thoroughly moisturizing on the skin. Oil-in-water emulsions can be rinsed off the skin without much effort. As a rule, emulsions of this type have high water phases. Examples of O/W emulsions are lotions, cleansers, and moisturizing creams.

For a water-in-oil emulsion, on the other hand, water droplets are encased by oil. Emulsions of this kind produce a greasy sensation on the skin's surface and can only be removed from the skin with the help of soap. W/O emulsions can be found in rich creams, such as hand creams that protect from the cold and dry heat in the winter.

Which one of the emulsion types you will create depends on the emulsifying agent used. As an example, glycerin stearate facilitates O/W emulsions.

Whether an emulsion turns out right—meaning whether or not the mixture will remain stable or separate again—can depend on many factors. Some emulsifying agents, for instance, will react sensitively to the presence of salt or a wrong pH. A few times, I've seen even already stable emulsions separate again after the last ingredient (in most of the cases, a preservative) was added. The processing temperature plays a role too: Both phases should always have the same temperature. Last, but not least, stirring speed and duration have to be watched— oftentimes, high shearing forces will be needed to properly distribute and disperse (mix) oil and water. However, as always, there are a few exceptions to this rule. Lanolin, for instance, won't hold up to too high shearing forces, so the water has to be added drop by drop.

Tip: **After the fact, it is often impossible to find out why an emulsion has separated again. For this reason, if you plan to develop your own recipes, I suggest keeping detailed notes on how you've worked. As a result, repetitive errors can be avoided, and you will later be able to recreate a good product.**

KULECZKA/SHUTTERSTOCK.COM

Scale. GRESEI/SHUTTERSTOCK.COM

Tools and Equipment

Before you can start concocting your first cream, in addition to the necessary ingredients, you will also need a few pieces of basic equipment:

Laboratory balance—Your most important tool is a precision scale with a gradation of 0.1 g (0.0035 oz) or, even better, 0.01 g (0.00035 oz). Precision or gold scales can be purchased for as little as $12, however, it is well worth it to invest in a more expensive model if you are looking for reliability and precision in performance. Never place your scales near electromagnetic fields, such as electrical outlets, because interferences may distort the results.

Beakers in different sizes—As basic equipment, two of the larger size [about 250 to 500 ml (8.5 to 17 fl oz) capacity] for the oil and water phases plus three smaller ones [about 50 to 150 ml (1.7 to 5 fl oz) capacity] for the active ingredients will suffice. I've had very positive experience with online shopping for beakers. You should thoroughly compare the various offers, though, because there might be significant price differences between them.

Mixing bowls or watch glasses for weighing smaller amounts

Glass stirring rods in different sizes, spatulas, double-sided measuring spoons, dropping pipettes, disposable syringes, small spatula

Immersion blender—make sure that the blending arm with head fits into one of your beakers

Milk frother or battery-operated stick blender for small amounts, or a special cosmetic grade electrical stirrer with different attachments

pH paper strips or pH indicator roll

Laboratory or candy thermometer

Ceramic mortar and pestle

Face mask to protect against particulate matter

Spray bottle containing 70 vol% alcohol for cleaning your work area (see page 20)

Containers for prepared cosmetics

Beakers. URFIN/SHUTTERSTOCK.COM

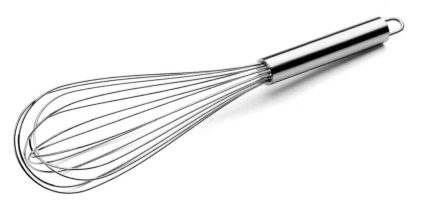

Wire whisk. IFONG/SHUTTERSTOCK.COM

Mixing bowls. PIRTUSS/SHUTTERSTOCK.COM

Spatula. ANDREW BURGESS/SHUTTERSTOCK.COM

Milk frother. EXOPIXEL/SHUTTERSTOCK.COM

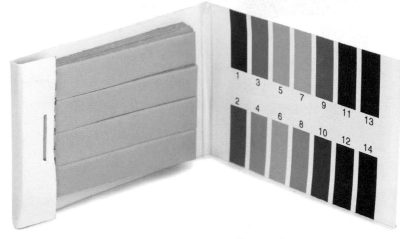

pH test strips. COPRID/SHUTTERSTOCK.COM

Stick blender with attachments. OLEJX/SHUTTERSTOCK.COM

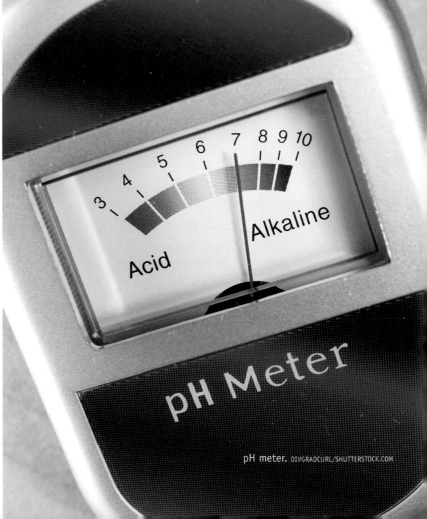

pH meter. DIVGRADCURL/SHUTTERSTOCK.COM

Mortar with pestle.
OLDAMULET/SHUTTERSTOCK.COM

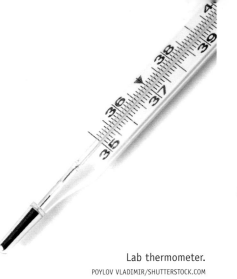

Lab thermometer.
POYLOV VLADIMIR/SHUTTERSTOCK.COM

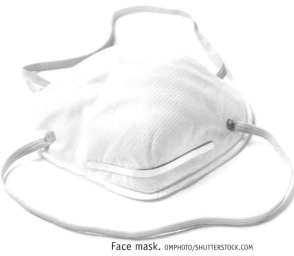

Face mask. OMPHOTO/SHUTTERSTOCK.COM

Spray bottle. GUZEL STUDIO/SHUTTERSTOCK.COM

Containers for prepared cosmetics. KUBAIS/SHUTTERSTOCK.COM

Your Workspace

One of the most important basic rules in skin care manufacturing is to keep sterile working conditions. Only sterile work will guarantee a long shelf life for your products! Especially with recipes containing a water phase, strict hygiene has to be maintained, since water will spoil considerably faster than oils. To sterilize your workspace, first remove everything nonessential to your manufacturing process from the working surface. Now, clean the working surface with water and standard commercial detergent, then spray it with alcohol (70 vol%; higher-grade alcohol is not necessary since the disinfecting properties stay the same). After the workspace has completely dried, cover it with paper towels or freshly laundered and dried dish towels.

HXDBZXY/SHUTTERSTOCK.COM

Wash your hands thoroughly with water and soap, then additionally apply hand disinfectant or rubbing alcohol. If you have sensitive skin, wear disposable gloves instead. Disinfect them before use and after every interruption, such as answering the telephone, or after you've touched something else.

Rinse all working utensils (including newly purchased ones), beakers, jars, and lids with hot water and place them bottom up onto paper towels to dry. Don't wipe any equipment with dish towels—doing so could cause contamination. After everything has dried, generously spray all vessels with alcohol and again leave upside down to dry.

It is also possible to sterilize equipment using a pressure cooker, as long as all of the materials are heat-resistant. PET containers, for instance, can melt and warp at a temperature only slightly more than 70°C (158°F).

To keep sterile spoons, spatulas, and similar utensils at hand, place them in a beaker filled with alcohol and remove when needed.

Last but not least: Never retrieve or dispense ingredients with your bare fingers. Always use a fresh spoon—namely, one fresh spoon for each new ingredient.

DIANA TALIUN/SHUTTERSTOCK.COM

Safe Working Conditions

The substances used to create cosmetics that will be applied directly onto the skin on an everyday basis are generally safe, but some precautions are still necessary. Some essential oils, for instance, are so highly concentrated they can even dissolve plastics. Therefore, essential oils should never come in contact with eyes or mucous membranes.

Manufacturing skin care products does involve marginal amounts of acids, such as lactic acid and citric acid. In undiluted form, acids can cause skin irritation, and a few drops of them will significantly alter the pH value of a cream.

Finally, there are various finely powdered ingredients that will envelop you in a cloud of particulate matter even when handled with reasonable care. An example for a powder of this kind would be sodium lauryl sulfoacetate (SLSA, see page 50). Inhaling it is very unpleasant and could cause long-term effects. Wearing a protective face mask is essential while working with powdered substances like this one.

For the above mentioned reasons, children and pets should be kept out of the workroom while manufacturing is in progress.

MELPOMENE/SHUTTERSTOCK.COM

Hobby or Small Business?

One or another hobby manufacturer of skin care products might after a while consider starting to sell their homemade products. Whether at a school-sponsored vendors' night or small craft fair, through a brick-and-mortar store or online, FDA regulations apply for all sales channels, and cosmetics may be sold only in compliance with current legislation. While the law does not require cosmetic products and ingredients (except color additives) to be manufactured to GMP specifications or get approved by the FDA before they can go on the market, cosmetics marketed to consumers on a retail basis (in stores, by mail order, or online) must meet ingredient labeling requirements under the Fair Packaging and Labeling Act and comply with other legislation regarding ingredients, testing, and packaging. If you want to further familiarize yourself with this topic, I recommend visiting the website of the U.S. Food and Drug Administration and considering their Small Businesses & Homemade Cosmetics Fact Sheet at http://www.fda.gov/Cosmetics/ResourcesForYou/Industry/ucm388736.htm#1.

PHOTOMIM/SHUTTERSTOCK.COM

ISTOCK.COM/MAXFX

Index of Raw Materials

Materials are listed by their common name(s) first, followed by their INCI (International Nomenclature of Cosmetic Ingredients) designation(s), which will help you to find the correct ingredient or to substitute for a proprietary blend if necessary.

Acetylated Lanolin Alcohol, Wool Alcohol, Wool Grease Alcohol, Sheep Alcohol

INCI: Lanolin Alcohol

Wool grease alcohol is an organic compound produced from the nonsaponifiable ingredients of lanolin, the fat of wool shearings (wool grease). It is an emulsifier for water-in-oil emulsions and sold in the form of small yellowish globules which, having a melting point between 58 and 65°C (136.4 and 149°F), can be processed and melted like regular wax.

Lanolin alcohol produces a less enveloping feeling on the skin than pure lanolin. It is markedly pH-stable, in both the acidic and alkaline basic range. Wool alcohol can bind six times its own weight in water, a property than can be even further enhanced by the addition of small amounts of beeswax or other waxes.

When processing wool grease alcohol, it is essential to ensure that the water phase and lipid phase both have the exact same temperature. Water has to be added to the lipid phase in small amounts to properly emulsify before adding in more water. Particularly pleasing creams can be created by combining lanolin alcohol with pure lanolin.

Wool alcohol balances the skin's lipid content and acts as a lubricant on the skin surface, giving the skin a soft, smooth appearance. It can be kept for approximately 18 months.

Algae Gel

INCI: Water, Propylene Glycol, Algae

Algae gel is derived from the red algae *Ahnfeldtia concinna,* a plant native to Hawaii. Red algae extract has an anti-inflammatory and firming effect on the skin and is thought to prevent and counteract premature skin aging. Recommended use levels are 5 to 10 percent.

Allantoin

INCI: Allantoin

Allantoin is a white, heat-resistant, and highly water-soluble powder. It occurs naturally in high concentrations in plants such as common comfrey *(Symphytum officinale)* and horse chestnut *(Cortex hippocastani)* bark. Because of its regenerating, moisturizing, and calming properties, allantoin is often used in formulations for treating blemished and irritated skin.

Almonds. ROMAN TSUBIN/SHUTTERSTOCK.COM

Almond Bran and Almond Meal

INCI: Almond Bran

Almond bran and almond meal are byproducts from almond oil pressing and are the residue of the dried, ripe seeds of sweet almonds after the oil has been expressed. They are used as mild exfoliating ingredients in body and face washing creams. Almond bran refines the complexion and is said to be especially effective for inflammatory skin diseases such as acne.

Almond Oil

INCI: *Prunus Amygdalus Dulcis* (Sweet Almond) Oil

Almond oil is a mild, well-tolerated, and very versatile oil. It can be used with all skin types and even for delicate baby skin. It is absorbed well into the skin and is able to transport other ingredients into the deeper skin layers.

Almond oil has a very limited inherent odor and so is especially suitable for aromatherapy cosmetics because it does not distort the scent of the essential oils.

When purchasing almond oil, it is well worth it to invest a little bit more and choose cold-pressed or food-grade oil. Cosmetics-grade almond oil is often diluted with sunflower oil, a fact frequently omitted from the package label. In natural cosmetics, sunflower oil being listed immediately after almond oil is a dead giveaway for diluted product.

Almond oil is also a good choice for oily extracts (macerates). However, the extract should be immediately used since almond oil, at least the cold-pressed variety, has only a limited shelf life.

Aloe Vera

INCI: *Aloe Barbadensis Miller*

Only the inner part of the leaf (the so-called aloe vera gel) is utilized. The outer (green) parts of the leaf contain substances which can irritate the skin and trigger allergic reactions. Aloe vera can come in vastly different qualities. The best gel is derived from plants allowed to grow without fertilizing and watering, resulting in a higher gel concentration. You should also take care to purchase pure aloe vera leaf gel without added conservants such as potassium sorbate and/or citric acid. A great alternative is freeze-dried, concentrated aloe vera powder (1:200).

Aloe vera has a cooling and anti-inflammatory effect. It is moisture-retaining and, when applied pure, makes an excellent remedy for sunburn and insect bites. Furthermore, it is believed to help clear the skin.

Apricot Kernel Oil

INCI: *Prunus Armeniaca* (Apricot) Kernel Oil

Apricot kernel oil is a very gentle oil that is well tolerated by sensitive skin. It has a smoothing and soothing effect and is readily absorbed. While its structure is similar to that of almond oil, apricot kernel oil is a little bit lighter. Very often, it is used in skin care products for babies.

Argan Oil

INCI: *Argania Spinosa* (Argan) Oil

Argan oil is derived from the fruit of the argan tree *(Argania spinosa),* endemic to Morocco.

The kernels of the fruit resemble olives and contain up to 50 percent of the light brown oil. To make 1 liter (33.814 fl oz) of oil, approximately 30 kg (66 lbs 4.9 oz) of fruit are needed. Because of the brittle wood of the argan tree, the fruit cannot be harvested mechanically through vibration, necessitating labor-intensive manual harvesting methods and making argan oil a precious commodity.

The astringent effect of argan oil and its ability to neutralize free radicals have a positive impact on connective tissue. Argan oil is also said to help with acne-prone, sensitive, and damaged skin.

Another noteworthy feature of the argan tree is that not only people value its crops! It makes for a truly entertaining spectacle when small goats, for which the fruits are a special treat, climb the branches of wild growing trees in pursuit of this delicacy.

Avocadin®

INCI: *Persea Gratissima* (Avocado) Oil and *Persea Gratissima* (Avocado) Oil Unsaponifiables

Avocadin® consists of the nonsaponifiable ingredients of avocado oil and is particularly helpful for barrier-damaged and dry skin. Recommended use levels are between 0.5 and 2 percent. Since Avocadin® has a comparatively high melting point, it should be melted together with heat-resistant oils and/or waxes in the lipid phase.

Avocado Oil

INCI: *Persea Gratissima* (Avocado) Oil

In its countries of origin, avocado oil is traditionally valued as a skin care product for protecting skin from dehydration. Rich in vitamins A and E, it contains up to 85 percent unsaturated fatty acids, mostly palmitoleic and linoleic acid. Its palmitoleic acid content is similar to that of sea-buckthorn berry oil or macadamia nut oil. It further contains a high percentage of unsaponifiable matter, meaning it has a high concentration of ingredients physiologically similar to the skin's own lipids. As a result, avocado oil is particularly helpful with improving cell regeneration and moisture content of the skin, fighting blemishes, and honing skin texture. Avocado oil is also used for the treatment of skin diseases, such as neurodermatitis or psoriasis. It can be easily applied onto the skin and is absorbed quickly.

Commercially available qualities of avocado oil include cold-pressed, instantly recognizable by its dark green color, and refined avocado oil, which is yellow.

Babassu Oil

INCI: *Orbygnia Oleifera* (Babassu) Seed Oil

Babassu oil is a precious oil, expressed from the fruits of the babassu palm *Orbygnia oleifera,* native to Brazil, which requires a costly harvesting process. The oil's fatty acid composition is very similar to that of coconut oil and in its virgin, meaning unrefined, state, it features a phenomenal fragrance.

Solid at room temperature, this oil consists mainly of saturated fatty acids. Upon contact with the skin, it will melt and get absorbed easily, making it ideally suitable for body butter. As an added bonus, it does not leave any greasy residue.

Babassu oil can be used for dry and chapped skin, as well as for oily or combination skin with blemishes and inflammations. Virgin babassu oil is vastly preferable over the refined variety.

Beeswax

INCI: Beeswax, Cera Alba (White), Cera Flava (Yellow)

Beeswax, a natural wax excreted by the wax-producing glands of honeybees, is used in the beehive for the building of honeycombs. The originally white wax scales will become progressively more yellow when mixed with pollen oil (a carotene-containing colorant found in the pollen transported by the bees) by the worker bee. Beeswax is sold in bleached and purified form under the trade name cera alba. It can be used in different cosmetics and soaps and also as a coating material for foodstuffs.

In cosmetics, it is mostly used as stabilizer. Its residue delicately envelops the skin with a pleasant protective coating, especially appreciated by those who suffer from chapped skin in the colder months. Caution should be exercised in people with pollen allergies, since even after the cleaning process, beeswax might still contain trace amounts of pollen residue, possibly inducing allergic reactions.

Bitter Almond Oil
(Hydrocyanic Acid Free)

INCI: *Prunus Amygdalus Amara* (Bitter Almond) Kernel Oil

Bitter almond oil is an essential oil smelling intensely of marzipan. Due to the strength of its scent, a carefully measured 0.5 percent amount of oil in the overall preparation will be sufficient for most recipes.

Borage Seed Oil

INCI: *Borago Officinalis* (Borage) Seed Oil

Borage seed oil is derived from the seeds of the annual herb borage (starflower) by cold pressing and, sometimes, subsequent refining. The cold-pressed grade is of golden yellow color with an herbaceous, cucumber-like fragrance, while refined oil is colorless to faintly yellow.

This oil is characterized by a particularly high gamma-linolenic acid content—up to 21 percent. On the other hand, borage seed oil does also have a few less desirable ingredients: Erucic acid, for instance, when used in larger amounts, can cause vascular damage. However, with less than 5 percent erucic acid, the nutritional and physiological value is still below the statutory limit amount for edible oils.

Borage seed oil is successfully used for treatment of atopic dermatitis, psoriasis, atopic eczema, and general skin regeneration. It can be found in more and more antiwrinkle creams, as well as in hair and nail care products.

On the minus side, borage seed oil can unfortunately be kept for only 10 to 12 weeks.

Broccoli Seed Oil

INCI: *Brassica Oleracea* (Broccoli) Seed Oil

Broccoli seed oil is of golden yellow, slightly greenish color, and has a subtle nutty odor. This markedly light, absorbent oil is mainly used in hair care products as biological silicone substitute. It improves the hair's combability without being greasy. In pure form, it can be used as split-end treatment—just rub a small amount into your palms and knead into the hair tips.

Cactus Pear Seed Oil, Prickly Pear Seed Oil

INCI: *Opuntia Ficus-Indica* Seed Oil

Cactus pear seed oil is a very high-priced commodity because its manufacturing process is especially costly and time-consuming. This oil prevents premature aging of the skin, tightens the skin, and reduces dark eye circles. It also has moisturizing and revitalizing properties and is beneficial for brittle fingernails.

Calendula Macerated Oil

INCI: *Calendula Officinalis* Flower Oil (and) *Glycine Soja* (Soy) Oil

Calendula oil is not classically pressed, but rather a macerated oil obtained by infusing botanical material into other oils, mostly soy oil. Calendula oil's yellow-orange color is caused by the carotin in the petals of the plant. The oil has wound-healing and anti-inflammatory properties and is often used to treat irritated skin. Recommended use levels are 2 to 10 percent.

Aloe vera. ISTOCK.COM/SMITT

Apricots. ISTOCK.COM/SARSMIS

Camellia Seed Oil, Tea Seed Oil

INCI: *Camellia Sinensis* Seed Oil

Camellia seed oil comes from the fruit of the tea plant *Camellia sinensis,* for which it is also often known as tea seed oil. Camellia seed oil has a similar chemical makeup to hazelnut oil, is quickly absorbed into the skin, and is used akin to olive oil in the geographic regions where it is grown.

Because it is capable of transporting active ingredients into the skin, tea seed oil is used for sensitive and dry skin as well as for skin prone to irritations. Geishas have been using camellia seed oil for ages as their secret for beautiful skin and shiny, voluminous hair.

Candelilla Wax

INCI: *Euphorbia Cerifera* (Candelilla) Wax

Candelilla wax is derived from the leaves and stems of the candelilla shrub of northern Mexico and the southwestern United States. The candelilla shrub is part of the Euphorbiaceae family, and the "wax" derived from it is very hard and of yellowish-brown color. The "wax" is not a wax at all: It consists of 18 to 20 percent resin, 5 to 6 percent crocusatin B, and 75 percent dotriacontane (unsaponifiable matter), making it technically a resin-hydrocarbon blend. Its melting point of 67 to 79°C (153 to 174°F) lies between the melting points of beeswax, which is also softer, and carnauba wax, which is harder.

Candelilla wax finds use in lipsticks, body melts, solid perfumes, and, at low dose rates, as stabilizer in emulsions. Three percent candelilla wax in a whipped shea butter will leave a very pleasant feeling to the skin and make application easier. It is also significantly more cost-effective than beeswax.

Carbamide

See Urea

Carnauba Wax

INCI: *Copernicia Prunifera* (Carnauba) Wax

The main purpose of this vegetable wax is to increase the thermal stability of such decorative cosmetics as kajal, mascara, or lipstick. Especially in waterproof makeup, carnauba wax is frequently used because the waterproof film created by it does prevent smudging of the makeup upon contact with water.

For some time now the wax, whose melting point at 82 to 85.5°C (179.6 to 185.9°F) is higher than that of beeswax, has also been utilized for skin and hair care products. It leaves the skin smooth and elastic, which is why it can be frequently found in antiwrinkle creams. As an ingredient in hair care products, it gives the hair shine and elasticity.

Avocados. KENISHIROTIE/SHUTTERSTOCK.COM

Beeswax. AFRICA STUDIO/SHUTTERSTOCK.COM

Borage. MATTEO SANI/SHUTTERSTOCK.COM

Carrageenan

INCI: Carrageenan

Carrageenan is a gelling agent extracted from the red edible seaweed *Chondrus crispus*. Of the different types of carrageenan, the one used for the recipes in this book is kappa 2-carrageenan, which creates strong, elastic gels. In order to do this, it needs to be processed at approximately 75°C (167°F), since carrageenan will not completely dissolve at lower temperatures. Its recommended use levels are from 0.1 to 1 percent.

Castor Oil, *Ricinus Communis* Seed Oil

INCI: *Ricinus Communis* (Castor) Seed Oil

Castor oil is a colorless high-viscosity oil. In my opinion, if used in too high concentrations, it has a rather dehydrating effect, even though I've frequently seen it used as an ingredient in bath oils for dry skin or eyelash care products. I only use it for iridescent lip gloss or lip balm recipes. Castor oil is widely used in soap manufacturing because it promotes sudsing.

Ceralan™

INCI: Lanolin Alcohol

Ceralan™ is a colorless and odorless waxy substance that is used to improve consistency and thermal resistance of emulsions and to prolong the shelf life of preparations. When used in oils, it acts as a gelling agent. It also has the ability to keep color pigments suspended, keeping them from settling to the bottom.

Cetostearyl Alcohol

INCI: Cetearyl Alcohol

Cetostearyl alcohol is a nonionic coemulgator and stabilizer, commercially available as small yellowish-white globules or pellets. Cetostearyl alcohol has a melting range of 48 to 53°C (118 to 127°F) and is melted together with the lipid phase.

Cetyl Alcohol

INCI: Cetyl Alcohol

Cetyl alcohol (palmityl alcohol) is a synthetically manufactured fatty alcohol sold in the form of small white platelets. In the recipes in this book, it is used as a stabilizer or coemulgator for emulsions and hair care products. One of the most remarkable properties of cetyl alcohol is its ability to influence the absorption characteristics of emulsions: Creams are absorbed faster into the skin and therefore produce less of a greasy feeling—a desirable property, for instance, in hand creams. It can also be used in emulsions for oily and blemished skin.

Cetyl alcohol is melted in the lipid phase. Its melting point is at 49°C (120°F), and recommended use levels are between 0.5 and 1 percent for dry skin and up to 3 percent for all other skin types.

Citric Acid

INCI: Citric Acid

Many of you might be familiar with the various household uses of citric acid. Depending on grade, it can serve as a gelling agent and preservative for jams or to decalcify household appliances.

Together with sodium bicarbonate, citric acid is the agent responsible for the fizzing action in bath essences.

Since direct contact with pure citric acid can irritate skin and respiratory tract, a face mask and gloves should be worn at all times when handling this ingredient. Citric acid is also strongly hygroscopic (tending to quickly absorb moisture from the air) and should therefore be kept in an airtight container at all times. The acid should also be kept out of reach of children and pets.

Cocoa Butter, Theobroma Oil

INCI: *Theobroma Cacao* (Cocoa) Seed Butter

Cocoa butter is the edible vegetable fat extracted from the the seeds of the cocoa plant. It is sold in different forms: The unrefined kind, with a strong cocoa odor, and the refined, deodorized variety with almost no noticeable scent. When deciding on either one of the two types, you should keep in mind that unrefined cocoa butter will remain strongly detectable even with higher perfume dosages. This might be tolerable when working with stronger fragrances such as vanilla scent.

Camellia. CLAUDIOVIDRI/SHUTTERSTOCK.COM

Castor oil plant. SALLY WALLIS/SHUTTERSTOCK.COM

Chamomile. IMAGES72/SHUTTERSTOCK.COM

For rose and similar delicate flower scents, however, it would be too overpowering. Cocoa butter is mostly sold as pellets, but also in blocks or in powder form.

Cocoa contains over 300 different substances. In Central American folk medicine, cocoa plays an important role and has a wide range of therapeutic indications. A recently discovered ingredient in cocoa is said to stimulate cell growth, smooth and prevent wrinkles—especially those around the mouth and eyes—as well as aid in wound healing.

In cosmetics, cocoa butter is utilized as a nurturing additive in creams, massage bars, body butter, and bath essences. It solidifies bar soaps and gives them a smooth texture, makes the skin soft and pliable, and is ideally suited for dry, stressed skin. Furthermore, it helps to prevent stretch marks and alleviate existing ones.

Liquified cocoa butter will need several days to regain its original firmness and snap. Overheating cocoa butter to more than 35°C (95°F) will convert its crystal structure to a less stable form with a reduced melting point—it will now melt even below room temperature and won't properly harden any more. Cooling it too fast, such as in the refrigerator, will also create an unstable crystalline structure.

Many people can develop allergic reactions to cocoa butter with age, which is said to be caused by certain proteins. Because of its notably high fat content, cocoa butter should also be avoided by people with oily skin or hypersecretion of the sebaceous glands. More than other oils, cocoa butter can contain LDL cholesterol, which is known to cause arteriosclerosis and heart attacks.

Coco-Betaine (CAPB)

INCI: Cocamidopropyl Betaine

Coco-betaine is a liquid surfactant of plant origin and also an emulsifying agent. As a very gentle surfactant, it conforms to natural and organic cosmetic standards. It has a good foaming ability, mild bactericidal effect (meaning it destroys bacteria), and is often used for baby products. Recommended use levels are 30 to 50 percent.

Coconut Cream, Coconut Milk

INCI: *Cocos Nucifera* (Coconut) Extract

Coconut cream has a skin nurturing effect akin to that of coconut oil, making the skin soft and pliable. In recipes, it may be substitued with coconut milk.

Coconut Oil

INCI: *Cocos Nucifera* (Coconut) Oil

Coconut oil is extracted from the kernel or meat of the coconut palm fruit and contains approximately 70 percent saturated fats. Having a melting point of approximately 23 to 26°C (73.4 to 78.8°F), coconut oil is solid at room temperature and therefore often also called coconut fat.

Coconut oil is absorbed quickly into the skin, albeit only superficially. It creates a nongreasy, cooling, and smooth skin feeling. However, coconut oil has comedogenic potential, meaning it can block the excretory ducts of the sebaceous glands. For this reason, with blemished skin, it should be avoided and replaced by babassu oil.

In cosmetics, coconut oil can be found in bath pralines, massage bars, lip balms, and hair care products. In India, coconut oil is traditionally used in daily body care routine. Women knead it into their hair to prevent it from being dried out by the sun.

Coffee Bean Oil, *Coffea Arabica Seed Oil*

INCI: *Coffea Arabica* Oil

The coffee plant, indigenous to the mountains of the southwestern highlands of Ethiopia, today is mostly grown in Central and South America. The fruits of the coffee shrub are about cherry-sized and green when unripe, turning from yellow to later red during the ripening process. In fully ripe condition, they are finally black-purple. Every fruit contains two kernels, known to us in their dried and roasted form as coffee beans.

Ripe coffee beans are harvested by hand and processed. There are two kinds of coffee oil: First, the oil of unroasted, raw coffee beans, light yellow in color and almost odorless, and, second, the oil of roasted coffee beans, which is what I use in my recipes. The latter is of a dark brown color and features the typical coffee aroma.

Coffee bean oil can be derived through extraction with diethyl ether or petroleum ether, or by CO_2 extraction. I prefer the CO_2 extract because, in solvent extraction, residues may still be present in the finished oil.

Coffee CO_2 extract contains caffeine, which makes it particularly suitable for stimulating cosmetics and those promoting blood circulation, such as anticellulite formulations.

Collagen

INCI: Hydrolyzed Collagen

Collagen is a structural protein in human connective tissue, where it occurs in virgin form. It improves moisture absorption and effectively decreases wrinkles. It should not be heated over 40°C (104°F). Recommended use levels are between 0.5 and 1 percent.

Cranberry Seed Oil

INCI: *Vaccinium Macrocarpon* (Cranberry) Seed Oil

Cold-pressed cranberry seed oil has a nutty scent and dark, golden yellow color. It is native to North America.

This active ingredient oil is relatively expensive. Recommended use levels for active ingredient oils should not exceed 10 percent in the finished product. Owing to its chemical composition, cranberry seed oil is perfectly suited to help restore dry, aging skin to its previous form. Its properties are similar to those of rosehip kernel oil. It produces a velvety feeling on the skin without leaving a greasy feeling. Cranberry seed oil soothes irritated skin and refines its complexion.

Cupuaçu Butter

INCI: *Theobroma Grandiflorum* (Cupuaçu) Butter

As can be gained from its Latin name, cupuaçu is closely related to cocoa. This tropical rainforest tree is common throughout the Amazon basin, and the cupuaçu butter is extracted from the bean-shaped seeds by cold pressing.

The butter is of light beige color, solid at room temperature, and has a fruity aromatic, sometimes slightly acidic, fragrance. It has a high phytosterol content, which regulates the lipid production of the skin and therefore its fat content. Furthermore, cupuaçu increases skin moisture, has an anti-inflammatory effect, and mild sun-protection properties.

Dead Sea Mud, Sea Silt Extract

INCI: Maris Limus

Dead Sea mud is very rich in minerals. It has a regenerating, cleansing, and balancing effect on the skin.

Citric acid. ICARMEN13/SHUTTERSTOCK.COM

Dead Sea Salt

INCI: Maris Sal

Dead Sea salt is very different from other salts on account of its extremely high content in minerals, such as sodium, iron, calcium, potassium, magnesium, manganese, sulfite, and many others. Dead Sea salt is mostly yellowish in color and feels wet to the touch.

A full bath with Dead Sea salt will improve circulation, tighten the skin, and stimulate the metabolism. It is also reputed to show drastic improvement for skin disorders, such as psoriasis and neurodermitis. Owing to its remarkable detoxifying effect, it is often used in cosmetics for blemished and oily skin.

How much of it is actually needed for a full intensive-action bath is highly debatable. Numbers vary between 200 g (7 oz) and 2,000 g (4 lbs 6.5 oz) of salt. My personal experience leads me to tend rather toward the latter.

D-Panthenol, Dexpanthenol, Provitamin B5

INCI: Panthenol

Panthenol or dexpanthenol, a precursor of vitamin B (provitamin B5), is actively involved in regenerative metabolic processes of the skin. This highly viscous, transparent, sticky liquid is well tolerated by the skin and used in many cosmetic products, such as healing ointment or diaper rash creams and other baby care products.

D-panthenol has a wound-healing, anti-inflammatory, and moisturizing effect; regenerates the skin; and improves its elasticity.

Recommended use levels are 1 to 5 percent for general applications, however not exceeding 2 percent as a cosmetic active ingredient; higher concentrations are reserved for therapeutic purposes, such as wound healing.

Since panthenol is heat-sensitive, it should always be processed at temperatures below 30°C (86°F).

Cocoa beans. JPC-PROD/SHUTTERSTOCK.COM

Elastin, Hydrolyzed Wheat Protein

INCI: Hydrolyzed Wheat Protein

Elastin for cosmetics manufacturing is plant-based and derived from wheat gluten. It improves the skin's elasticity, alleviates wrinkles, and has a regulating effect on the acid mantle. Elastin is used in both hair and skin care products. In hair care products, it envelops the hair as a fine film, giving it shine and volume. It will dissolve in hot or cold water. Recommended use levels are from 0.2 to 1 percent.

Coconut. TOBIK/SHUTTERSTOCK.COM

30

Emulsan

INCI: Methyl Glucose Sesquistearate

Emulsan is an emulsifying agent. It can be used in a variety of products and is extremely pH-tolerant, which makes it particularly useful since it will process well with nearly all ingredients. Emulsan may be used in creams, lotions, emulsifying scrubs, and many other preparations. The optimal fat content for creams is between 20 and 40 percent, and for lotions and cleansing creams around 15 to 25 percent. Emulsan is an O/W emulgator with a recommended use level between 3.3 and 8.2 percent for creams.

The way an emulsan-containing cream will later feel to the skin greatly depends on the way it has been processed. For best results, emulsan should be handled as follows: The lipid phase (containing the emulsan) and the water phase should have a temperature between 70 and 80°C (158 and 176°F). To facilitate proper emulgation, the lipid phase should be added into the water phase in small amounts and stirred with an immersion blender at the highest possible speed as long as possible.

Essential Oils, Ethereal oils

INCI: Essential Oils

Essential or ethereal oils are important plant components, giving plants their fragrance and taste.

Different methods can be employed to extract these fragrant compounds from plants, the most commonly used ones being vapor distillation, expression and extraction with the help of solvents, CO_2, or—for particularly fragile plants—fatty substances (enfleurage). Oils harvested with the CO_2 extraction method contain more and other ingredients than those resulting from distillation, which are more pungent and have a different smell. When alcohol is used as solvent in liquid-liquid extraction, the resulting extract is called "absolute."

Essential oils, when inhaled, can influence our mood, powers of concentration, stress level perception, and other emotions, sending signals to the limbic system of our brain through our sense of smell. Applied onto the skin, essential oils will stimulate nerve endings and so transmit messages to our brain. A few drops of peppermint oil, for example, can help cure a headache when massaged into the temples. Never underestimate the sometimes potent effects of essential oils: Some oils can induce contractions in pregnant women or even trigger seizures in epileptics. Therefore, as a general rule for essential oil concentration, 1 drop essential oil to 10 ml (0.338 fl oz) of prepared product—2 drops per 10 g (0.353 oz) for body cosmetics—should never be exceeded. Alcohol-based perfumes should contain no more than 5 percent essential oils, solid perfumes no more than 10 percent. My suggestion to you: When not completely sure, seek expert advice or consult a good reference book.

Tip: Store essential oils at consistent room temperature in dark-colored bottles and reduce oxygen content in the vapor space of the vessel by adding argon gas or glass beads to decrease evaporation.

Ethanol/Ethyl Alcohol

INCI: Alcohol

Since ethyl alcohol does not contain added denaturants, making it suitable for human comsumption and therefore usable for the manufacture of foods, it is considerably more expensive than "cosmetic base water" (a diluent consisting of 95 to 96 vol% denatured alcohol, perfume, and panthenol).

Natural cosmetics can be preserved exclusively with the help of ethanol. For this, between 10 and 15 vol% ethanol computed to the water phase will be needed. If at least 12 percent alcohol is used to preserve, the emulsion will keep for 8 to 12 weeks. Ten to 12 percent will preserve it for 4 to 6 weeks; however, the ethanol percentage should never fall below 10 percent. Alcohol has disinfecting and cooling properties, but also a dehydrating effect. You skin will tell you how much alcohol is necessary for preserving. If at 10 percent you already perceive a strongly dehydrating sensation, replace a portion of the alcohol with potassium sorbate.

Besides ethanol, you may also use alcoholic tinctures or extracts as preservatives. Just keep in mind that these mostly contain only 70 vol% alcohol, making it necessary to adjust the weight in the recipe accordingly.

A little sample calculation
100 g (3.527 oz) emulsion with 30 percent lipid phase and 70 percent water phase:

To yield 70 g (2.469 oz) 15 vol% preserved water phase, you will need 9.2 g (0.325 oz) 95 vol% alcohol and 60.8 g (2.145 oz) water phase.

To yield 70 ml (2.367 fl oz) 15 vol% preserved water phase, you will need 15 ml (0.507 fl oz/0.451 oz) 70 vol% alcohol and 55 ml (1.860 fl oz)/55 g (1.940 oz) water phase.

Evening Primrose Oil

INCI: *Oenothera Biennis* (Evening Primrose) Oil

The evening primrose, also fever plant, is native to eastern and central North America and was introduced to Europe about 400 years ago. The oil is cold pressed from the seeds, which contain about 27 percent oil. Thanks to large amounts of linolenic and gamma-linolenic acid (GLA), evening primrose oil is one of the few oils reputed to successfully help in treating neurodermatitis and psoriasis.

Nonrefined evening primrose oil will unfortunately keep for only a very limited time. It is often sold adulterated with tocopherol (vitamin E).

Extracts/Tinctures

INCI: Extract

The recipes in the book use either water-hydroalcoholic or propylene glycol–based extracts. Extracts always consist of a solvent (here, alcohol or propylene glycol) and vegetative material with its oil- and water-soluble components extracted. Alcoholic extracts have the added benefit of acting as preservatives, ensuring a longer shelf life for the finished product. Most commercially available extracts have an alcohol content of 70 percent.

Here are a few examples of extracts: *Nettle* stimulates circulation and hair growth and is vasodilative. It is used in dandruff shampoos and skin creams for blemished skin. *Calendula/marigold* has a calming, smoothing, and healing effect, and is good for severely strained skin and skin in need of extra care. *Thyme* has cleansing and disinfecting properties, and is helpful with blemished skin and acne. *St. John's wort* is helpful for wound healing, for instance in acne. Applied pure, it is helpful for burns and insect bites. *German chamomile* has healing, calming, and anti-inflammatory properties and a nurturing effect, and is especially suitable for sensitive and children's skin. *Hamamelis* has astringent action and a toning effect for sensitive, blemished, and large-pored skin. *Green tea* clears the complexion and soothes stressed skin. *Cucumber* is moisturizing and clearing for blemished skin. *Da zao (jujube fruit or Chinese date)* moisturizes and intensifies the skin's stress resistance. *Jasmine* has a soothing and clearing effect. *Neem* is used in shampoos to soothe itching and to remove and prevent head lice. *Saline* is anti-inflammatory and astringent, for oily and blemished skin.

Facetensid HT

INCI: Disodium Laureth Sulfosuccinate

Facetensid HT is a markedly gentle surfactant often used in baby shampoos. It consists of plant-based ingredients (citric acid and fatty alcohols). Although Facetensid HT contains 41 percent tensides, it may nevertheless be used in higher dosages (up to 50 percent). You can substitute with another disodium laureth sulfosuccinate–based mild surfactant.

Fluid Lecithin CM

INCI: Lecithin, *Glycine Soja* (Soy) Oil or *Helianthus Annuus* (Sunflower) Seed Oil (soy alternative)

Fluid lecithin CM is an emulsifying agent consisting of 50 percent lecithin and 50 percent soy oil, and it is yellowish brown in color and of syrup-like consistency. With fluid lecithin CM, you can create O/W as well as W/O emulsions, depending on the ratio of the oil and water phases. Water amounts of up to 50 percent will in most cases result in a W/O emulsion; proportions of more than 65 percent water will form an O/W emulsion. A big drawback of this emulsifying agent is that, in most cases, the prepared end product will have retained the heavy characteristic lecithin odor. Fluid lecithin should be used in quantities between 5 and 12 percent; when added as a nurturing coemulgator, 0.5 to 3 percent.

German Chamomile Oil

INCI: *Chamomilla Recutita (Matricaria)* Flower Oil

There are two types of chamomile—German (Hungarian, wild, or genuine) chamomile and English (Roman, garden, true, or common) chamomile. German chamomile is also called blue chamomile because its essential oil can be recognized by its blue color, resulting from the formation of the hydrocarbon azulene (in Spanish, "azul" means "blue") during vapor distillation. There is only one other essential oil with this characteristic blue coloration: The oil of *Achillea millefolium*, commonly known as yarrow. German chamomile has a calming, herbaceous fragrance, while the yellow to golden Roman chamomile oil sports a sweetish scent.

The most characteristic feature of German chamomile is its anti-inflammatory and wound-healing effect. In cosmetics, it aids with blemishes, acne, and other inflammatory processes of the skin. German chamomile oil is also a popular ingredient in skin care products for babies and children. When blended with tangerine and honey, German chamomile has an especially pleasant odor. German chamomile oil is very expensive: about $12 for 5 ml (0.169 fl oz).

There is also a fatty oil marketed under the name of chamomile oil. This oil is a macerate, meaning chamomile blossoms have been left to soak in oil for several weeks until the oil has been "infused" with the fat-soluble elements of the chamomile. The probably best-known example for an oil produced by this method is St. John's wort oil. Macerates can be easily prepared under home conditions (see Macerates).

Ghassoul

INCI: Lava Clay

Ghassoul, or rhassoul, naturally found and organically mined from deposits in the Atlas Mountains of Morocco, is of black-brown color and known under the trade name lava clay. This name does not originate in its consisting of volcanic rock, but rather comes from the Latin word "lavare," for washing. Lava clay comes in different colors and is sold under various names: Red, green, pink, or white clay; kaolin; healing chalk; and many others.

Ghassoul and other types of lava clay are valued for their extraordinary absorption qualities, binding large amounts of water and other liquids, as well as for their extractive abilities, making them a frequent ingredient in clarifying face masks.

Glycerin

INCI: Glycerin

Also called glycerol or glycerine, glycerin is a clear, highly viscous liquid without any characteristic odor. As a skin-identical ingredient (a natural component of the skin's own moisturizing system), it is usually very well tolerated and especially recommended in preparations for dry skin.

In cosmetics manufacturing, the humectant glycerin is often combined with other emollients, such as urea or sodium lactate. Used in overly large dosages, however, particularly in conjunction with gelling agents, glycerin will produce a sticky feeling on the skin; therefore, recommended use levels should not exceed 5 percent.

Because of its ability to reduce the surface tension of the substances to be emulsified, glycerin is a frequently used ingredient in shower gels, hair shampoos, and cleansing products. It can be kept for approximately 2 years.

Coffee beans. GUTEKSK7/SHUTTERSTOCK.COM

Cranberries. ALEXANDER LEONOV/SHUTTERSTOCK.COM

Evening primrose. IAN GRAINGER/SHUTTERSTOCK.COM

Glyceryl Stearate (GMS)

INCI: Glyceryl Stearate, Glyceryl Stearate Citrate

Glyceryl stearate is a compound emulsifier and emulsion stabilizer. It can be used to make oil-in-water and water-in-oil emulsions, depending on the percentage of the oil and water phase: Less than 50 percent oil phase will result in an O/W emulsion, more in a W/O emulsion. As an ingredient in creams, glyceryl stearate creates a very pleasant, thoroughly moisturized skin feeling. However, these creams have a marked film-forming effect so that I personally prefer to use this ingredient mostly for night creams. Best results are obtained with a lipid phase around 35 percent.

Processing is uncomplicated: The emulgator is heated together with the oil to 65°C (149°F). Then water, boiled to 65°C (149°F) and cooled, is gradually stirred into the lipid phase. Recommended use levels are from 4 to 5 percent. Glyceryl stearate is a great coemulgator for pH sensitive emulsifying agents like glyceryl stearate SE or Tegomuls®.

Glyceryl Stearate SE

INCI: Glyceryl Stearate SE

This emulgator is especially well suited for very light formulations, such as day creams with lipid phases between 20 and 30 percent or cleansing creams. Glyceryl stearate is plant-based and somewhat difficult to work with. It will not tolerate prolonged high shearing forces; after no longer than 2 minutes of mixing with an immersion blender, additional manual stirring is required until it has cooled down. Unfortunately, it is also very sensitive to acids and will react poorly to some preservatives. The most reliable preserving method is using alcohol or alcoholic extracts. On the plus side, this emulgator will reward you for all your extra efforts with a sensational feeling on the skin.

Grape Seed Oil

INCI: *Vitis Vinifera* (Grape) Seed Oil

Grape seed oil works well as a base oil for oily skin and combination skin. It quickly penetrates the skin and makes it supple without leaving any greasy residue. It also regulates sebaceous production.

Cold-pressed grape seed oil is of green-golden color and rich in linoleic acid and natural lecithin. When properly stored in cool and dark surroundings, grape seed oil can be kept for approximately 9 months.

Hazelnut Oil, Hazel Seed Oil

INCI: *Corylus Avellana* (Hazel) Seed Oil

Hazelnut oil is commercially available in different qualities. Cold-pressed hazelnut oil is golden yellow with a slightly nutty fragrance, while the oil of the roasted nuts is of a somewhat darker and slightly brownish color and smells intensely of hazelnut.

Hazelnut oil is an optimal skin care product and also ideally suitable as massage oil. It provides relief for various skin problems, particularly those of sensitive and dry skin. This very nourishing oil is absorbed slowly, making it a true blessing for the skin, especially in cold weather.

Hazelnut oil is a regular component in a variety of cosmetic products; for instance, in lipsticks, massage oils, and cold creams.

Hemp Oil

INCI: *Cannabis Sativa* Seed Oil

Hemp oil, or hemp seed oil, is obtained by pressing the seeds of the hemp plant. Among other benefits, hemp oil is known for its remarkable skin tolerance. With internal as well as external application, it produces very good results, especially in neurodermitic skin, thanks to its high content in gamma-linolenic acid (GLA), comparable amounts of which are otherwise only found in evening primrose and borage seed oil. Hemp oil contains more than 80 percent unsaturated fatty acids, which, on the minus side, significantly reduces its shelf life. For this reason, the oil should be stored tightly sealed in a cool, dark place.

When creating your own recipes with this ingredient, make sure to mix it with oils high in oleic acid, such as almond, hazelnut, and avocado. This will have a stabilizing effect and prolong the shelf life of your finished hemp oil product.

Honey

INCI: Honey

Using honey for skin care purposes is an age-old tradition. Besides its antibacterial and moisturizing effects, it also stimulates circulation and acts as a cleanser. When applied in the form of a freshly prepared mask (such as with yogurt and oil), it gives the skin a silky-soft feeling.

Especially noteworthy is manuka honey, which contains methylglyoxal, a strong disinfecting ingredient with antibacterial effect. When purchasing honey, look for organic-grade because conventional honey will often contain traces of antibiotics. Furthermore, the honey should be cold extracted since many of its valuable ingredients will be destroyed by heat. For this reason, honey should only be used in temperatures below 40°C (104°F).

Hyaluronan

INCI: Hyaluronic Acid

Hyaluronan or hyaluronic acid is a complex sugar that is naturally present in the human skin.

It is sold as white powder which will turn into a gel when dissolved in water. Because of its ability to act as a moisturizer and visually tighten skin, it is a popular ingredient in many antiaging products.

Hyaluronic acid is not inexpensive, but the cost is offset by its recommended use level of a moderate 0.1 to 0.5 percent. The powder can be somewhat difficult to work with because of its tendency to lump when directly added to the water phase. The most effective option for mixing is to carefully disperse (thoroughly mix) the powder in a small amount of alcohol and then stir the resulting mixture into the water phase.

Hydrolates

INCI: Hydrosol

Hydrolates, or hydrosols, also known as floral waters, are distillates—products from steam distilling plant materials—often created as a byproduct during essential oil production. They contain all of the plant's water-soluble substances as well as a limited amount of essential oils. Floral waters are the cooled condensate from the fragrant water originally steamed with the plant material after the stronger essential oils have been separated, containing all the plant's essence in a milder form.

The probably best-known hydrolate is rose water, often used in marzipan manufacturing. When you purchase hydrolates, make sure they are genuine hydrolates. The nongenuine (fake) rose water is just water perfumed with essential oil. While noticeably cheaper, this substitute rose water is not nearly as effective as the genuine product.

Grapes. IROOM STOCK/SHUTTERSTOCK.COM

Hazelnuts. 2CREATIVE/SHUTTERSTOCK.COM

Honey. FFOLAS/SHUTTERSTOCK.COM

Jasmine. TOLIKOFF PHOTOGRAPHY/SHUTTERSTOCK.COM

Jojoba. CASEY K. BISHOP/SHUTTERSTOCK.COM

Lavender. NISHIHAMA/SHUTTERSTOCK.COM

Because hydrolates can, unfortunately, very quickly become contaminated by germs, a preservative is often added. I personally prefer the 100 percent pure form. When you have larger amounts you don't plan to work with right away, you may safely freeze the hydrolates for later use.

Here, a few key words about the hydrolates referred to in this book:

Cornflower Hydrolate

INCI: *Centaurea Cyanus* Hydrolate

Scent: Hay with a light citrus note

Effect: Decongestant. Soothes tired, swollen eyes, regenerates and revitalizes the complexion, tones tissue.

German Chamomile Hydrolate

INCI: *Chamomilla Recutita* Hydrolate

Scent: German chamomile

Effect: Anti-inflammatory and calming. Alleviates reddened and irritated skin.

Jasminum Sambac Hydrolate

INCI: *Jasminum Sambac* Hydrolate

Scent: Intensive-flowery

Effect: This hydrolate is mostly used because of its scent, which can have a mood-lifting and stress-relieving effect.

Lemon Hydrolate

INCI: *Citrus Limonum* Hydrolate

Scent: Lemon

Effect: Removes blackheads and refines pores.

Neroli (Orange Blossom) Hydrolate

INCI: *Citrus Aurantium* Flower Hydrolate

Scent: Flowery

Effect: Calming and moodlifting.

Rose Hydrolate

INCI: *Rosa Damascena* Hydrolate

Scent: Rose

Effect: Astringent and firming. Effectively decreases wrinkles and helps the skin regenerate.

Tea Tree Hydrolate

INCI: *Melaleuca Alternifolia* Hydrolate

Scent: Fresh, spicy

Effect: Antibacterial and detoxifying.

Witch Hazel Hydrolate

INCI: *Hamamelis Virginiana* Hydrolate

Scent: Aromatic-flowery

Effect: Cleanses and tightens skin, refines pores, and improves circulation.

Jojoba Oil

INCI: *Simmondsia Chinensis* (Jojoba) Seed Oil

Jojoba oil is not an oil in the traditional way, but instead a liquid wax ester extracted from the seeds of the evergreen jojoba shrub growing in the American Sonora Desert.

Cold-pressed jojoba oil is of golden yellow color and almost odorless, making it indispensable as a base oil, especially in aromatherapy. For cosmetics, it is universally usable, since it is suitable for all skin types and is also antiallergenic. With characteristics close to those of the human sebum, the wax easily mixes with the skin's sebum. This creates a thin lipid envelope which retains and regulates skin moisture, leaving the skin smooth and pliable. Jojoba oil does not leave any greasy residue. It strengthens the connective tissue, prevents wrinkles, and aids the healing process in sunburn. It has a sun protection factor of 4.

Jojoba oil will keep virtually indefinitely, making it a beneficial addition in blends with other oils that are more susceptible to oil degradation.

Kaolin (White Lava Clay)

See Ghassoul

Lactic Acid (80 Percent)

INCI: Lactic Acid

Lactic acid naturally occurs in the hydrophobic lipid envelope of the human skin. Together with other substances, it preserves the skin's acid mantle. In cosmetic preparations, it is mostly used in very small dosages to adjust the pH value. Recommended use levels are between 0.1 and 1 percent.

Lamepon® S (Collagen Surfactant)

INCI: Potassium Cocoyl, Hydrolyzed Collagen

Collagen surfactant is a nonionic surfactant from glucose obtained from corn and fatty alcohols from coconut and palm kernel oil, which is combined into a mild surfactant together with hydrolyzed collagen. It is of pale to dark yellow color and has a pH of 6 to 7.

Collagen surfactant is remarkably mild and hypoallergenic while also having excellent foaming abilities. As a primary surfactant, it is highly suited for use in mild shower gels, shampoos, and wash lotions.

Lamepon® S contains 30 percent surfactants, and recommended use levels are up to 80 percent in a surfactant blend.

Lamesoft®

INCI: Coco-Glucoside (and) Glyceryl Oleate

Lamesoft® is a very mild and effective cleanser, naturally derived from coconut (coco-glucoside) and sunflower oil (glyceryl oleate). It can be found mostly in blends with Plantapon® SF, where it acts as a thickening agent. It is used as part of a surfactant system and as refattener in shampoos, shower gels, bath formulations, and baby products.

Lanolin

INCI: Lanolin

Lanolin, also known as wool wax or wool grease, is secreted by the sebaceous glands of sheep and protects the wool fiber of their coats. It is viscous, of yellowish brown color, and has a characteristic, although not unpleasant, smell of sheep. Lanolin can bind many times its own weight in water and is a good emulgator for creams with a high lipid phase, such as cold creams. However, manufacturing of this type of cream is very time-consuming because the liquid has to be added in manually, drop by drop. To avoid phase separation, the mixture needs constant stirring until it has completely cooled.

Lanolin is easily absorbed into the skin and makes it pleasantly soft. Its melting point is at 40°C (104°F), and it will keep for 1 year or more. Here, too, organic-grade quality is preferrable to avoid product from pesticide-treated sheep. Pesticides might have been deposited in the skin and have contaminated the lanolin. If you intend to purchase your lanolin at the pharmacy, keep in mind that there is another product with a very similar name, lanolin DAB—this is not pure lanolin, but a mixture of 65 percent lanolin, 15 percent paraffin, and 20 percent water. Recommended use levels for lanolin are usually at 3 to 8 percent, for salves up to 50 percent.

Lanolin Substitute

INCI: Oleic/Linoleic/Linolenic Polyglycerides

Lanolin substitute is a viscous mass resembling liquid honey. It consists of polyglycerin fatty acids derived from sunflower oil and is soluble in water as well as in oil. Lanolin gives lip gloss a beautiful luster and can also be used as a moisturizing coemulgator in creams.

Recommended use levels in creams are 2 to 10 percent, in balms 2 to 30 percent.

Laureth-4

INCI: Laureth-4

Laureth-4 is a synthetically derived liquid emulsifier used in bathing oil and oily bath essence formulations. It is fat-soluble and has very good cold emulsifying properties. Recommended use levels are between 5 and 20 percent. In my opinion, 5 percent is completely sufficient. Since laureth-4 is colorless and almost odorless, it is often preferred over lysolecithin.

Lavender Essential Oil

INCI: *Lavendula Augustifolia* (Lavender) Oil

Lavender oil is one of the the most popular essential oils. Its scent has a calming and anti-inflammatory effect and stimulates circulation. Lavender oil is one of the few essential oils that can be applied pure. It is proven to help with insect stings and burns. Applied pure to a wasp bite, it will prevent swelling and significantly reduce pain. Even in extensive burns—such as from spilled hot liquids—I have noticed that lavender oil will noticeably accelerate the healing process.

Lipodermin

INCI: Water, Lecithin, Alcohol, *Carthamus Tinctorius* (Safflower)

Lipodermin is made up of liposomes, microscopically small globules of lecithin which are hollow inside. Because their structural composition closely resembles that of skin cells, the liposomes contained in Lipodermin are able to carry antiwrinkle agents, vitamins, or plant extracts into deeper skin layers (into the stratum corneum). The phosphatidylcholine in Lipodermin concentrate is derived from soy and can be added to cosmetics, such as creams, body lotions, and shower gels, as a nurturing and moisturizing ingredient and as antiwrinkle agent. It has also proven effective for blemished skin, where it is applied pure directly onto affected skin areas.

Recommended use levels are 15 to 30 percent in products for blemished skin, 5 to 10 percent when used as an antiwrinkle agent.

Low-Luster Pigment, Ronaflair™

INCI: Mica (A: >50 percent); CI77120 (Barium Sulfate) (B: 25–50 percent); CI 77891 (Titanium Dioxide)

Low-luster pigment (LLP) consists of fine mica coated with a mixture of barium sulphate and titanium dioxide, enabling the material to diffuse light. Using this functional filler in makeup and tinted moisturizers will visibly minimize wrinkles. Recommended use levels are 1 to 10 percent.

Lysolecithin

INCI: Lecithin (E322)

Macadamia nuts. SOMMAI/SHUTTERSTOCK.COM

Lysolecithin is a plant-based emulgator derived from soy. It has a viscous consistency and a brownish color. Because of its emulsifying properties, it can be used in bath essences of various types, but is also popular as a nurturing additive for shower gels and shampoos.

Lysolecithin is cold-processable. Drawbacks are its color and the slight but peculiar odor, which is perceived as unpleasant by some people. Lysolecithin can be used to prevent "bathtub rings," which can be caused when no other emulsifying ingredients (such as milk powder and/or honey) are part of the formulation.

For bath essences (oil baths, shower melts, bath pralines), recommended use levels are approximately 10 percent.

Because lysolecithin is prone to oxidation, it should be stored tightly sealed in a cool, dark place. Under these conditions, it will keep for 18 months.

Macadamia Nut Oil

INCI: *Macadamia Ternifolia* Seed Oil

Macadamia nut oil is expressed from the nut meat of the macadamia tree. The nuts contain 70 percent oil. Macadamia nut oil is of pale yellow color, smells slightly nutty, and tastes very good. It is an especially popular ingredient in massage oils because it is able to transport other ingredients (such as essential oils) into the skin and gets absorbed quickly. Macadamia nut oil has a regenerating and smoothing effect and is notably recommended for dry and chapped skin.

Mangos. INACIO PIRES/SHUTTERSTOCK.COM

Macerate (Oily Extract)

Macerates are extracts of fresh or dried plant parts steeped in oil. Ready-to-use macerates are often soy oil based because this oil is inexpensive.

If you want to prepare your own oily extract, I recommend using olive or jojoba oil as carrier oil.

Marigolds. WASANAJAI/SHUTTERSTOCK.COM

To yield 500 ml (17 fl oz) oil, you will need approximately 250 g (8.8 oz) dried or 750 g (26.5 oz) fresh plant parts. Keep in mind that when using fresh plants, the oil will turn rancid faster because of the higher water content.

Preparation is simple:

Cold extraction: Place the finely cut plant parts in a tall glass jar with tight-fitting lid. Fill the jar up to the rim with olive or jojoba oil and keep it on a sunny windowsill for 3 weeks. Then strain the oil through a cloth diaper or piece of cheesecloth, pressing out excess liquid. Discard the used plant parts.

Now, using the extracted macerate but fresh plant parts every time, repeat the procedure another 3 to 4 times, shaking the container daily. Depending on the desired concentration, your macerate (last plant parts discarded) will be ready to use after 3 to 6 weeks.

Heat extraction: For this method, put the finely cut plant parts, together with the oil, into a bowl (preferably a glass one) and place it into a saucepan with boiling water. Keep the mixture in this water bath for approximately 3 hours. As with cold extraction, here, too, the oil has to be strained through a piece of cheesecloth and excess liquid pressed out. After having repeated this procedure another 3 to 4 times, discard the remaining plant parts as well.

Macerates are best stored in airtight brown glass bottles, which will prolong their shelf life.

Magnesium Stearate

INCI: Magnesium Stearate

Magnesium stearate is a nonpoisonous magnesium salt. This finely ground white powder is added to powder and makeup formulations to keep components from separating.

Mango Butter, Mango Seed Butter

INCI: *Mangifera Indica* (Mango) Seed Butter

The mango tree, which can reach an age of many hundred years, is one of the oldest crop plants. Native to India and Burma, it has been cultivated for 4,000 years and is now grown in all tropical and subtropical countries.

After the mangos have been sun dried, their hard shells are cracked by hand to reach the tiny seeds, from which the butter is obtained by solvent extraction with hexan and subsequent refining. Mango butter is ivory colored and has a mild scent.

Mango butter has regenerating and healing properties and balances the skin's lipid content. It gives a very special texture to body butter, body melts, and lip balm. Mango butter makes the skin soft and pliable, and dry hair can benefit as well from the positive properties of this ingredient.

Mango butter is often used in the manufacture of high-quality soaps and as substitute for paraffin. Stored in a cool place, it will keep for about 1 year.

Medium Chain Triglycerides (MCT) Oil (Neutral Oil)

INCI: Caprylic/Capric Triglyceride

Neutral oil is a nonirritant, oxidatively stable oil that is easy to spread on the skin and gets quickly absorbed without leaving any greasy residue. It is especially suited for sensitive or neurodermitic skin since it does not penetrate into the deeper skin layers and therefore won't interact with the lipids from the skin's own protective layer. MCT oil is most comparable to squalane, with which it can be substituted.

Melissa Oil, Lemon Balm Oil

INCI: *Melissa Officinalis* Oil

Almost everybody knows this perennial herb, and many grow it in their garden or on their balcony. Even though lemon balm grows vigorously and is by some gardeners even considered a weed, *Melissa officinalis,* or genuine melissa essential oil, is one of the most expensive oils on the market today. The reason: To produce 1 liter (33.8 fl oz) of the essential oil through vapor distillation, 7,000 kg (15,432 lbs) of plant material are needed. Just 1 ml (0.034 fl oz) essential oil costs between $17 and $23. Two cheaper oils, often also—wrongly—called melissa oil, are frequently used to adulterate lemon balm oil: citronella essential oil *(Melissa indicum)* and lemon grass oil *(Cymbopogon citratus)*. Their combined scent is similar to, but cannot compete with, the subtle aroma of genuine lemon balm oil.

Lemon balm has been utilized as a medicinal plant for more than 2,000 years. Its fungicidal and antimicrobial properties and powerful antiviral effect are used to treat herpes infections, eczema disorders, and for general wound healing. Today, it is also frequently used in aromatherapy.

On an emotional level, lemon balm has a mood-lifting, refreshening, and harmonizing effect. Its delicate aroma soothes the nerves and helps with insomnia, and it is equally popular as a relaxing massage oil and for oil baths.

Melissa (lemon balm). UBONWAN POONPRACHA/SHUTTERSTOCK.COM

Milk Powder

INCI: Whole Dry Milk

Today, a great variety of powdered or dried milk is available—cow's milk, skim milk, whole milk, yogurt, whey, and buttermilk powder are offered. There are also sheep's and goat's milk in powdered form, both of which have a significantly higher fat content and are ideally suited for various types of bath essences.

Especially for people with skin problems, goat's milk, so rich in vitamins and minerals, is a true indulgence. Its linoleic acid has a positive impact on growth and functioning of the cell structure. Sheep's milk contains vitamins A, D, and E and has a soothing effect on the skin.

Those who like it even more sumptuous may want to try mare's or donkey's milk. Mare's milk is a little easier to come by than donkey's milk, and both are said to help with atopic eczema when used internally or externally. Those who have a chance to visit the Netherlands should set out to hunt for the variety of powdered milk available there—if you are lucky, you might find such exotic products as camel's or elk's milk in an affordable price range.

Montanov™ S

INCI: Coco-Glucoside, Coconut Alcohol

Montanov™ S is a natural coemulsifying agent used to maintain the stability of emulsions.

It creates a creamy texture in a surfactant environment and increases the foaming capacity of preparations. Coconut alcohol is dissolved in the hot water phase. Recommended use level: 1.5 percent.

Milk powder. SKYHYUN/SHUTTERSTOCK.COM

Nettles. NADA B/SHUTTERSTOCK.COM

Olives. TETXU/SHUTTERSTOCK.COM

Papaya. BUPPHA/SHUTTERSTOCK.COM

Peaches. JIANGDI/SHUTTERSTOCK.COM

Natural Moisturizing Factor (NMF)

INCI: Water, Sodium Lactate, Lactic Acid, Glycerin, Serine, Sorbitol, TEA-Lactate, Urea, Sodium Chloride, Lauryl Diethylendiaminoglycine, Lauryl Aminopropylglycine, Allantoin, Denatured Alcohol

The Natural Moisturizing Factor (NMF) is found within the corneocytes, and makes up 20 percent to 30 percent of the dry weight of the stratum corneum. It consists of amino acids (40 percent), sodium PCA (12 percent), lactate (12 percent), urea (7 percent), ions (18.5 percent), sugars (8.5 percent), and a few other things. These are the natural water-soluble humectants of our skin. One of the roles of skin care products is to mimic our skin's natural moisture barrier. Adding elements of the NMF to our products will give the skin a fresh, toned appearance; reduce small wrinkles; and supply the skin with moisture.

Neem Oil

INCI: *Azadirachta indica* Seed Oil

Neem oil has antibacterial, fungicidal, and antiviral properties. Because of the triterpenoide azadirachtin it contains, neem oil can be employed as a natural insecticide and for the treatment of plant diseases. Neem oil can also be utilized as a natural remedy against pests and parasites in humans and animals alike. In cosmetics, it can be used in the manufacturing of various products such as creams, soaps, lotions, and nail oils. Please be cautious: Orally ingested neem oil can lead to acute poisoning, even in small amounts.

Oat Protein

INCI: Oat *(Avena Sativa)* Protein

Oat protein, after drying, creates a velvety-smooth protective film on the skin, alleviates wrinkles, enhances skin resistance, and maintains and regulates skin moisture.

Olivem® 900

INCI: Cetearyl Olivate, Sorbitan Olivate

Olivem® is a natural emulsifying system for W/O cosmetic formulations. Developed from natural olive chemistry, it is particularly well tolerated by the skin. It functions well in the manufacturing of creams with a very high lipid phase (more than 50 percent) and rich oil gels (oil content between 70 and 90 percent). Olivem® is a good alternative to lanolin and wool grease and is also similarly processed: The oil and water phases are initially heated to 80°C (176°F), then water is added drop by drop to the lipid phase and mixed in. Additional water is only added after the water has been completely emulsified. While cooling, the emulsion has to be constantly stirred to prevent phase separation. Recommended use levels for Olivem® are from 10 to 13 percent in the lipid phase for creams and up to 30 percent in oil gels. Creams formulated with this emulgator balance the skin's lipid content and feel enveloping without appearing sticky.

Olive Oil

INCI: *Olea Europaea* (Olive) Fruit Oil

No other oil is as well-known as olive oil—a bottle of it can be found in almost any kitchen. In cosmetic use, the same rule applies as for dietary purposes: Only cold-pressed olive oil specifically marked "extra virgin" has all the good properties attributed to olive oil. For this reason, when purchasing, take care only to buy "extra virgin" quality.

Olive oil has a tradition as carrier oil for macerates, the most well-known being the deep red St. John's wort oil. Because of its anti-inflammatory effect, olive oil is also often used as base oil for healing ointments. Thanks to its relatively high tocopherol content, it is suitable for long-time storage and can be kept for up to 2 years.

Since olive oil is only very slowly absorbed and softens the skin, it is especially useful for chapped, flaky skin conditions. Applied to incrustated wounds, if softens the scab and considerably speeds up healing.

Those who perceive olive oil's inherent odor as too strong may mix it with equal parts macadamia nut oil, which will neutralize its scent.

Optiphen

INCI: Phenoxyethanol (and) Caprylyl Glycol

Optiphen is a paraben-free preservative performing equally well in the alkaline and acidic pH range.

Use levels from 0.5 to 1.5 percent and a processing temperature up to 60°C (140°F) are recommended. Products preserved with Optiphen will keep for approximately 6 months.

Papaya Oil, Papaya Seed Oil

INCI: *Carica Papaya* Oil

The enzyme papain contained in papaya products reputedly helps to soften and break down dead skin cells and particles without damaging skin areas with intact circulation. Papaya oil is easily absorbed and good for oily, blemished, and acne-affected skin. It strengthens hair and gives it shine by preventing it from drying out.

Paraben K

INCI: Methyl Paraben, Propyl Paraben, Benzyl Alcohol

Paraben K is a blend of two organic cosmetics grade preservatives and an antimicrobial fragrance.

By their chemical composition, parabens are a series of parahydroxybenzoates or parahydroxybenzoic acid esters. Glucosides and esters of parahydroxybenzoic acid naturally occur in almost all spices and plant pigments. There is also an insect, the great diving beetle, which produces a paraben-like substance within its own body. Living in a constantly wet environment, the beetle uses this substance to keep mildew pathogens at bay.

Paraben K should always be added when recipes call for protein-containing ingredients, such as milk derivatives, collagen, or elastin. Methyl and propyl paraben are most effective in a neutral pH-range (between pH 6 and pH 8).

One drop Paraben K per 10 g (0.353 oz) prepared cosmetic product will ensure a shelf life of approximately 6 weeks; doubling the concentration to 2 drops Paraben K per 10 g (0.353 oz) prepared product will increase its shelf life to 3 months. Protein-containing creams will keep only for half that time; plan batch sizes accordingly and prepare only as much as can be used up before it will expire.

Peach Kernel Oil

INCI: *Prunus Persica* (Peach) Kernel Oil

The peach is native to northwest China and came to Europe via Persia, from which it got the species name, *persica*. Peach kernel oil, derived from the seed of the peach kernel through solvent extraction, is pale yellow in color and smells faintly nutty with a hint of almond. Since its effect on the skin is similar to that of almond kernel oil, peach kernel oil is often used to stretch this more expensive oil. Peach kernel oil helps with dry, flaky, or chapped skin and also has many benefits for mature skin.

Perlatin

INCI: Glycol Distearate, Sodium Laureth Sulfate, Cocamide MEA, Laureth-10

Perlatin is a pearlizing wax dispersion that gives shampoos, shower oils, and shower gels a pleasant mother-of-pearl shine. Recommended use level is 2 percent.

Phenonip

INCI: Phenoxyethanol, Methylparaben, Ethylparaben, Butylparaben, Propylparaben, Isobutylparaben

Phenonip is a liquid synthetic preservative which will inhibit microbial growth in your homemade cosmetics, making them safe for long-term storage (for up to 2 years). It is very easy to work with and relatively impervious to heat. Phenonip may be used in a pH range from pH 3 to pH 8 and can be processed together with almost any other ingredient. Recommended use levels vary between 0.25 and 1 percent. For aqueous bath essences and shampoos, 0.25 percent is sufficient. Higher concentrations are only needed for preparations that are by their nature difficult to preserve, as in formulations with high protein content. For emulsions (O/W as well as W/O), the manufacturer recommends use levels between 0.4 and 0.7 percent. Phenonip can be easily mixed into a cold or warm emulsion.

Phytolanolin

INCI: Oleic/linoleic/linolenic polyglycerides

Phytolanolin is a plant-based alternative to lanolin. It gives lip gloss a beautiful shine and ensures that the gloss stays put on the lips.

Piroctone Olamine, Octopirox

INCI: Piroctone Olamine

Piroctone olamine is a mild chemical substance often used in anti-dandruff shampoos, treatments, and sprays. It is thought to fight oily and dry dandruff as well aid hair prone to quickly reacquire an oily sheen.

Plantapon® SF

INCI: Sodium Cocoamphoacetate (and) Glycerin (and) Lauryl Glucosid (and) Sodium Cocoyl Glutamate (and) Sodium Lauryl Glucose Carboxylate

Plantapon® is a mild, purely plant-based, ready-to-use surfactant that conforms to natural and organic cosmetic standards. It has almost no inherent odor, making it particularly useful for only lightly perfumed formulations, such as child care products. It has excellect foaming abilities and cleanses the skin without dehydrating. Recommended use levels are 20 to 50 percent in products for adults and 20 to 30 percent in children's formulations. You can use it equally well for shampoos and for shower gels. Because of its very low viscosity, it is often used in combination with Lamesoft® PO 65 [INCI: Coco-glucoside (and) Glyceryl Oleate]. For this purpose, adjust the pH of the product to pH 5 to pH 6 and add 1 to 3 percent Lamesoft® to your recipe. To improve texture, you may also enhance your formulation by adding 1 percent salt (rock salt).

PNC 400

INCI: Sodium Carbomer

This synthetic polymer can be used as a thickener and suspending agent in cosmetic products, most notably to manufacture crystal clear viscous gels. It does not leave a filmy residue on the skin, as can often be noted with xanthan. PNC 400 is not pH-sensitive; however, it should not be predispersed in alcohol since it does not react well with it.

Powdered Pearl

INCI: Margarita Powder

Pearl powder slows down the skin aging process and is used as an antiwrinkle agent. Powdered pearl can be simply stirred into the prepared formulation. Recommended use levels are between 1 to 3 percent.

Propylene Glycol, Propylene Glycol USP

INCI: Propylene Glycol

Propylene glycol is a synthetically manufactured, clear, colorless, and nearly odorless liquid that is also strongly hygroscopic. It is soluble in water and alcohol, but not in oil. Like sorbitol, propylene glycol is a moisturizing agent with additional preserving properties, but only in use levels of over 20 percent in the water phase.

Prune Kernel Oil, Plum Kernel Oil

INCI: *Prunus Domestica* Seed Oil

The best feature of cold-pressed prune kernel oil is definitely its scent. It smells of almonds and marzipan, and very intensely at that, which makes it especially useful for manufacturing marzipan-flavored lip balms or lip exfoliants (with oil and sugar). Smacking lips is in this case explicitly encouraged!

Like apricot kernel oil or peach kernel oil, plum kernel oil is obtained from the soft inner kernel of the plant. Softening the skin and protecting it from free radicals, it is especially beneficial for the delicate skin around the eyes and lips. Thanks to a high content of tocopherol and unsaturated fatty acids, it will last up to 1½ years when properly stored.

Rewoderm®

INCI: PEG-200 Hydrogenated Glyceryl Palmitate, PEG-7 Glyceryl Cocoate

Rewoderm® is a very mild, skin-friendly, nonionic surfactant, used as viscosity regulator for other surfactants. It consists of coconut and palm oils and, despite acting as a liquid thickener, is not highly viscous itself. In the manufacturing process, Rewoderm® is gradually added at the very end until the product has reached the desired consistency. Because Rewoderm® will continue to set, in some cases the final product may turn out thicker than expected. Should this ever happen, just add some more water to the mixture.

Recommended use levels for Rewoderm® are 1 to 4 percent; surfactants account for 70 percent. Rewoderm® has a pH of 7 to 8.

Plums. SHULEVSKYY VOLODYMYR/SHUTTERSTOCK.COM

Prickly pears. JOHN COPLAND/SHUTTERSTOCK.COM

Rice Bran Oil

INCI: *Oryza Sativa* (Rice) Bran Oil

Rice bran oil is made from vitamin-rich rice bran, the byproduct remaining when brown rice is polished. The bran contains between 16 and 32 percent oil, which is derived through solvent extraction and refining.

Rice bran oil has a relatively long shelf life (up to 12 months) and is especially suitable for irritated, sensitive skin. Due to the natural sun-protection action of the gamma-oryzanol contained in rice bran oil, this oil is a popular ingredient in sunscreen products. In Japan, rice bran oil is regarded as a traditional beauty aid.

Rosehip Kernel Oil (Wild Rose Oil, *Rosa Canina* Fruit Oil)

INCI: *Rosa Canina* Fruit Oil

The wild rose—commonly known as the dog-rose—originally came from Chile. It thrives in heights up to 3,000 m (about 10,000 feet) and grows in Europe as well as in the temperate regions of America, Asia, and Africa. Its marvelously bright orange-red colored fruits are, strictly speaking, only pseudo-fruit. The actual edible parts are in fact the edgy, light-colored, rock-hard nutlets from which the oil is extracted during a rather costly procedure. Not every common oil press is able to withstand the marked toughness of the nutlets. To strip the kernel of its tough outer shell, the Chileans utilize, as I have been told, a special shelling device developed by a German engineer. If the sturdy outer shell has not been properly removed before the pressing process, the resulting oil will be recognizable by a characteristic scorched scent. Therefore, whenever possible, buy this oil only after having smelled a sample. If conducting an olfactory test is not feasible, rely on a reputable dealer.

Rosehip kernel, or wild rose, oil is either sold in unrefined form, usually red-orange in color and with a fruity smell, or refined, which is lighter-colored and less odorous.

Rosehip kernel oil contains all-transretinoic acid, which accelerates the skin renewal process. Thanks to collagen formation, it enables dry skin to retain more moisture, protecting it this way from drying out. It also reduces pigmentation and moderates scarring. With all these features, wild rose oil is a wonderful facial oil, especially for dry and aging skin. When stored cool and protected from light, wild rose oil can be kept for up to 12 months.

Rügen Healing Chalk

INCI: Calcium Carbonate

Rügen healing chalk is a pure natural product containing calcium carbonate, magnesium carbonate and silicon, iron, and aluminum compounds. Because of its chemical composition, healing chalk possesses increased thermophysical properties, meaning it has a warming effect and will hold its temperature. It stimulates and speeds up the skin's circulation and metabolism. The skin is gently cleansed and nurtured and becomes noticeably smoother. Added to washing creams, healing chalk acts as a gentle abrasive and, used internally, binds toxins before they are expelled from the body.

Please note: Healing chalk should be avoided by those with kidney disease or kidney-related problems.

Safflower Oil

INCI: *Carthamus Tinctorius* (Safflower) Seed Oil

Safflower oil is pressed from the seeds of the safflower. It features a markedly high content of linoleic acid. It also contains alpha-tocopherol, vitamins A and K, and up to 1 percent nonsaponifiable ingredients.

Safflower oil is an ingredient optimally suited for oily skin. It is quickly absorbed, very light, and does not leave any residue. For blemished, severely oily skin, a mixture of safflower oil, hemp, or black currant seed oil, grape seed oil, and babassu oil is recommended. The vitamin K contained in safflower oil is also said to help with reducing dark circles.

Sea-Buckthorn Berry Oil

INCI: *Hippophae Rhamnoides* Berry Oil

Until 1980, the former Soviet Union had been the leading manufacturer of sea-buckthorn berry oil; today, China tops the ranking with a cultivated area of 1 million hectares (2.47 million acres).

Quantity, however, does not equal quality, and the finest quality sea-buckthorn berry oil is produced by Mongolia, where the shrubs are not cultivated, but rather grow wild.

There are three kinds of sea-buckthorn oil: seed oil and two types of fruit oil.

1. **Cold-pressed fruit oil:** Sea-buckthorn berry oil obtained from freshly pressed juice by centrifugation or cold pressing.

2. **Seed oil:** The kernels are separated from the pulp and then cold pressed or extracted to make sea-buckthorn seed oil.

3. **CO_2-extracted fruit oil:** Dried sea-buckthorn berries are crushed while the kernels remain intact. Liquidized carbon dioxide pulls the oils out while retaining the beneficial nutrients in the berry.

Sea-buckthorn berry oil is dark to orange-red because of the carotenoids it contains, has a sweetish-fruity scent, and aromatic taste. This oil contains particularly large amounts of palmitoleic acid, which is also a natural component of human skin fat. Palmitoleic acid reduces wrinkles and can delay the signs of skin aging, a benefit especially valued for dry and chapped skin.

Sea-buckthorn berry oil protects the skin from free radicals, UV radiation, and harmful pollutants from the environment. It strengthens the skin's own immune mechanisms, firms the dermal tissue, and alleviates already-existing wrinkles.

When deciding between cold-pressed and CO_2-extracted oil, I always recommend opting for the cold-pressed variety. If cold-pressed oil from fresh—not dehydrated—berries is available, this is the best choice of all: You will be rewarded with a wonderfully fruity and intense sea-buckthorn aroma that can't be matched by dried berries.

Rosehips. JAN BERODES/SHUTTERSTOCK.COM

Sesame Oil

INCI: *Sesameum Indicum* (Sesame) Seed Oil

Sesame seed oil is obtained by pressing the seeds of the sesame plant. Initially originating in Africa and regarded as one of the oldest oilseed crops known, today this annual plant has been naturalized in India, China, Burma, and Mexico. The seeds grow in capsules containing 80 to 100 seed kernels each. Since the capsules have staggered ripening times, harvesting is mostly facilitated by hand.

Just as with hazelnut oil, sesame seed oil comes in different forms, made either from unroasted or from roasted/toasted seeds. Cold-pressed oil from unroasted seeds is pale yellow with a subtle sesame scent; the oil of toasted seeds is amber-colored and smells of popcorn. For use in natural cosmetics, cold-pressed sesame oil from unroasted seeds is preferred because it has a longer shelf life than refined oil and also a more unobtrusive inherent odor.

In India, sesame oil is regarded as a principal skin care product and, unlike our own custom, applied before taking a bath. The Ayurvedic technique of Gandusha (oil pulling) uses unroasted oil for daily oral hygiene: Prior to brushing, a tablespoonful of oil is slowly moved around in the mouth, then pulled through the teeth, which has a detoxifying effect. As an added benefit, this procedure enhances the sense of taste, eliminates bad breath, strengthens the gums, and reduces tooth decay.

Sesame oil is also used for oil massages and Shirodhara "third-eye" oil stream treatments.

Internally applied, sesame oil is known to lower blood pressure and reduce cholesterol levels.

Safflower. KPG_PAYLESS/SHUTTERSTOCK.COM

Sage. DIANA TALIUN/SHUTTERSTOCK.COM

Sea-buckthorn.
VALENTINA RAZUMOVA/SHUTTERSTOCK.COM

Sea salt. CYRICK/SHUTTERSTOCK.COM

Its secondary plant compounds (lignans sesamin and sesamolin) act as potent antioxidants and are used in the treatment of tumors. Next to ghee (clarified butter), sesame oil is generally regarded as the best natural detoxicant.

In cosmetic formulations, sesame oil is used as base oil for dry and poorly circulated skin.

It absorbs quickly and is therefore an ideal carrier oil for transporting other ingredients, such as essential oils, into deeper skin layers.

When stored in a cool and dry place, sesame oil can be kept for up to 12 months.

Shea Butter

INCI: *Vitellaria paradoxa* (Shea) Butter

Shea butter (also known as karité or ori) is extracted from the seeds of the African shea tree, which is common from western Africa to the Upper Nile region. Shea trees grow in locations where other oil palms are unable to thrive due to limited precipitation.

To make shea butter, the outer pulp is removed from the collected fruits to expose the oil-rich nuts, which are then either sun dried or desiccated in special drying ovens and ground in oil mills. Hulls are sifted out with a coarse sieve so that only the nuts remain. The completely shelled nuts are then extracted in a stove and afterward crushed by hand with mortars and pestles, producing an oily mass. This paste is mixed well by hand under addition of water to help separate out the butter oils until it is almost white in color, a sign that all impurities and foreign particles have been removed. More water is evaporated from the resulting extract by boiling; then the shea butter is finally filtered, cooled to harden, and packaged.

Unfortunately, this traditional method of producing unrefined shea butter has been mostly replaced by industrial refining, in which the shea nut paste is heated to more than 100°C (212°F), yielding significantly more product, but destroying valuable nutrients in the process. Refined shea butter is pure white and odorless. Unrefined shea butter has a yellowish, sometimes also a grayish or greenish, color and a slightly nutty, often distinctively smoky, aroma, which by some can be perceived as unpleasing.

Shea butter contains up to 11 percent nonsaponifiables, which is very beneficial for the functioning of skin, making it pliable and preventing it from drying out.

In clinical studies, 15 percent shea butter cream has been proven to be more efficient than cortisone ointment in the treatment of skin disorders such as eczema or dry, aging skin. Shea butter is very well tolerated and can be found as an ingredient in a variety of cosmetic products. It is also used to prevent stretch marks and for breast care while nursing.

A particularly noticeable advantage of shea butter is its airy, creamy consistency, resembling whipped cream. It can be whipped cold together with a small amount of jojoba oil, producing wonderful body butter. Shea butter should only ever be heated very gently [never exceeding 35°C (95°F)] to prevent it from becoming grainy, meaning that the formerly creamy vegetable butter may resolidify with a sandy consistency after having been melted. You will recognize this when the butter feels as if there were tiny sand grains in it. Should this have happened despite greatest care, it can be remedied by gently remelting the butter, then continuously stirring while cooling.

Silicon Dioxide

INCI: Silica

Silicon dioxide is the only gelling agent suitable for manufacturing of clear oil gels. There are two different kinds of silica. The type used in this book has a very small particle size and is able to absorb large amounts of moisture. Since it is extremely fine and lightweight, it should only be handled while wearing a face mask. With a capability of absorbing up to 40 percent of its own weight in moisture without losing its flowability, silicon dioxide is valued as an anticaking agent and often used to improve the spreadability of powdered cosmetics. When purchasing silica (silicon dioxide), make sure not to confuse it with siliceous earth—these are two different products!

Silk Powder, Serica, Micronized Silk Powder

INCI: Serica/Silk powder

Serica, or silk powder, is the finely pulverized silk thread of the mulberry silkworm's cocoon.

A single cocoon yields about 3,000 to 4,000 m (3,281 to 4,374 yards) of silk thread.

Silk powder can be used to minimize the oily sheen in body butter for a gently matting effect.

Micronized silk powder is used in decorative powder cosmetics such as mineral powder and eye shadow.

Silk Protein, Hydrolyzed Silk

INCI: Hydrolyzed Silk Protein

Silk protein, derived from silk fibers, is a popular ingredient for antiwrinkle preparations and also an effective moisturizer. Hydrolyzed silk is used for products where the silk is dissolved into the water phase, such as shampoos and lotions. Recommended use levels are 1 to 5 percent.

Silk White, Extender W

INCI/CI (Color Index): Mica, CI 77891 (Mica and Titanium Dioxide)

Silk White, a blend of mica and titanium dioxide, is a powdered pigment with a slight mother-of-pearl shimmer. Lightweight and with a high volume, it is used as a filler and consistency enhancer. Not to be confused with pure mica, which by some manufacturers is called silk mica.

Sodium Bicarbonate/Baking Soda

INCI: Sodium Bicarbonate, Sodium Hydrogen Carbonate

Bicarbonate of soda is one of the main ingredients in bath bombs and can be found in the baking aisle of the supermarket under its common name, baking soda. Why add baking soda to one's bath water at all? First of all, it is slightly alkaline and thus softens the water. More important, however, is the effervescent effect in water it produces in conjunction with citric acid.

Two other commercially available common substances are often confused with sodium bicarbonate because of the similarity in their names: The highly caustic sodium hydroxide (NaOH) is used in soap production and should under no circumstances be added to bath essences. Washing soda, or sodium carbonate, also known as soda ash, is utilized as a detergent and is equally out of place in cosmetics manufacturing.

Sodium Lactate

INCI: Sodium Lactate

Sodium lactate, the sodium salt of lactic acid, is, together with urea and glycerin, one of the components of the skin's Natural Moisturizing Factor (NMF). It has two main purposes: Firstly, in combination with lactic acid, it acts as a pH buffer in formulations containing urea and, secondly, thanks to its own hydrating action, it can also be used in recipes without urea, in conjunction with lactic acid alone. Application concentration will depend on the form it is available in: Powdered sodium lactate is used at a rate of 1 percent sodium lactate to 0.5 percent lactic acid (80 percent).

Sodium Lauryl Sulfate, Sodium Laureth Sulfate, Sodium Lauryl Ether Sulfate

INCI: Sodium Lauryl Sulfate, Sodium Laureth Sulfate, Sodium Lauryl Ether Sulfate

Known as SLS, or SLES, it is an anionic detergent and surfactant found in many cosmetic products. It has an antibacterial and antiviral effect. In salves, lotions, and dishwashing liquids, it is used as an emulgator.

Sodium Lauryl Sulfoacetate (SLSA)

INCI: Sodium Lauryl Sulfoacetate

SLSA is a powdered surfactant of natural origin that conforms to natural and organic cosmetic standards. It has excellent cleansing and foaming abilities, does not dehydrate the skin, and is mild and safe for most skin types. SLSA is mainly used in solid or powdered bath products, such as bubble bars, bath bombs, bath powders, and shampoo bars. The recommended use level is around 50 percent.

Please note: When handling SLSA, a face mask should be worn at all times since the fine powder generates dust and irritates the respiratory tract.

Sodium Pyrrolidone Carboxylic Acid

INCI: Sodium PCA

Sodium PCA is the sodium salt of pyroglutamic acid which occurs naturally in human skin, accounting for 12 percent of the skin's own Natural Moisturizing Factor (NMF). Sodium PCA is an excellent humectant. If used on its own, recommended use levels are between 2 and 5 percent. When combined with other hydrating ingredients, such as glycerin, urea, or sodium lactate, 0.5 to 2 percent is sufficient.

Soy Oil, Soy Acid

INCI: *Glycine Soja* (Soy) Oil

Soy oil belongs to the small group of oils containing significant amounts of alpha-linolenic acid.

Besides this, soy oil contains isoflavones (phytoestrogens), making it a popular ingredient in medicinal and pharmaceutical products. Soy oil is water-emulsified and rehydrating, retaining moisture in the skin's horny layer. Of all plant-based oils, it has the highest lecithin content, which makes it a good coemulsifying agent and balances the skin's lipid content.

In body care products, soy oil predominantly serves as a carrier oil for liposoluble plant-based ingredients and vitamins. Since it is absorbed into the skin rapidly and finishes residue-free, soy oil can be used as a base for bathing oils and creams. It also protects the skin from loss of moisture. Cold-pressed soy oil can be kept for up to 9 months when stored in a cool environment.

Squalane, Phytosqualan®

INCI: Squalane

Squalene is one of the main components of the sebum and the hydrolipidic film, of which it constitutes 12 percent. It is sourced from shark liver, but plant-derived squalane (*note the different spelling for plant-sourced oil*) is now available. Phytosqualan® is a plant-derived squalane obtained from the unsaponifiable fraction of olive oil pomace. Being an odor- and colorless, completely stable, transparent oil, squalane is perfectly adapted to cosmetic preparations.

For recipes with oil and water phases, squalane is part of the lipid phase. It softens and smoothes the skin without leaving a greasy feeling, making it a coveted ingredient for light face creams. Based upon its natural affinity with the skin and ability to penetrate easily, squalane helps emulsions to be absorbed into the skin more easily.

Since squalane lowers the viscosity of emulsions, plan your recipes to contain sufficient amounts of solid fats and/or waxes to counterbalance when use levels exceed 5 percent.

St. John's Wort Oil

INCI: *Hypericum Perforatum* Oil

St. John's wort oil is not a plant oil in the conventional sense, but rather an oily extract (macerate) of plant parts from St. John's wort—mostly from the blossoms. Traditionally, it is used as a base for olive oil extracts.

As home remedy, St. John's wort is known for its soothing and healing effects, for instance in rheumatism, lumbago, and gout, but also for sprains and bruises.

As skin care ingredient, its soothing and healing effect brings relief especially to dry, but also to inflamed, skin. However, because of its photosensitizing effect, St. John's wort should not be applied to skin areas that will later be exposed to sun rays; it increases the skin's photosensitivity to an extent that might lead to sunburn-like symptoms, such as redness or swelling.

Sesame seeds. AGUSTIN ESMORIS/SHUTTERSTOCK.COM

Sucrose Cocoate, Sanfteen

INCI: Sucrose Cocoate

Sucrose cocoate, a surfactant manufactured from sucrose ester and coconut fatty acid, is known in Europe under its trade name Sanfteen, popularized through the 1974–2004 German TV program *Hobbythek* and affiliated DIY books. It has an ointment-like consistency and smells of soap. Its mildness and ability to reduce the irritative effects of other surfactants make it a great additive in baby care products. At temperatures higher than 27°C (80.6°F), sucrose cocoate will liquefy.

Sucrose cocoate contains 65 percent washing-active substances; recommended use levels are 1 to 5 percent.

Shea butter. LUISA PUCCINI/SHUTTERSTOCK.COM

Surfactant Blend

INCI: Disodium Laureth Sulfosuccinate, Cocamidopropyl Betaine, Sucrose Cocoate

This surfactant blend, introduced by the 1974–2004 German TV program *Hobbythek*, consists of different, mutually compatible surfactants: 60 percent Facetensid HT or other disodium laureth sulfosuccinate–based surfactant, 35 percent coco-betaine, 5 percent sucrose cocoate. The surfactant blend has a surfactant content of between 39 percent and 41 percent.

Titanium Dioxide, Titanium Oxide, Titanium White, TiO2

INCI: Titanium Dioxide (CI 77891)

Titanium dioxide is an opaque white powdered pigment of mineral origin. Used in comparatively large quantities in mineral foundation recipes, it can be dispersed in water as well as in oil. Not to be confused with Silk White.

Tocopherol (TCP)

See Vitamin E

St. John's wort. SCISETTI ALFIO/SHUTTERSTOCK.COM

Urea (Carbamide)

INCI: Urea, Carbamidum, Carbonyl Diamide

Urea, like glycerin, is a component of the skin's own moisturizing factors (Natural Moisturizing Factor, or NMF) and can be found in the horny layer (stratum corneum). The urea used in this book's recipes, however, is synthetically derived. While this synthetic ingredient is not approved for use in natural cosmetics, it is very well tolerated by the skin.

Urea is very heat-sensitive and tends to disintegrate quickly. You will detect possible degradation by a pungent smell of ammonia, which can be counteracted by buffering the mildly acidic emulsion with sodium lactate and lactic acid. This is especially important when using pH-sensitive preservatives, such as potassium sorbate, since the decomposition process will slightly increase the preparation's pH. However, formulations containing urea should be used up after 4 weeks at the latest.

Urea has also another interesting property: It works as an enhancer, aiding other water-soluble ingredients in reaching deeper skin layers.

Recommended use level for nonmedicinal formulations are between 2 and 5 percent, sufficient for a moisture-retaining effect. Because urea is heat-sensitive, it should be predissolved in a small amount of cold water and only stirred into the lukewarm preparation at the very end of the process.

Urea is one of the best moisturizing ingredients. Similarly to plant-based emulgators, such as hydrogenated palm glyceride (sold as Tegomuls® in Europe), it produces a comparatively dry, soft feeling on the skin, including with higher lipid phases.

Vitamin C

INCI: Ascorbic Acid

Vitamin C has a regenerating and healing effect in damaged connective tissue and can also be used for inflamed and blemished skin. Combined with tocopherol, it helps in the treatment of age spots. Vitamin C inhibits collagen degradation and stimulates connective tissue metabolism.

Vitamin C is very sensitive to oxygen. For this reason, preparations containing vitamin C should be stored in airtight containers. In aqueous solutions, vitamin C disintegrates quickly, which can be counteracted by acidification of the pH or by stabilizing the emulsion with a gelling agent.

Thyme. IRES003/SHUTTERSTOCK.COM

Witch hazel. SHUTTERSTOCK.COM

Vitamin E/Vitamin E Acetate, Tocopherol

INCI: Tocopherol, Tocopheryl Acetate

In skin care preparations, vitamin E is used chiefly for its antioxidant properties. When added in the proper concentration (5 percent), it prolongs the shelf life of fat- and oil-containing formulations. Vitamin E acetate is much more stable than vitamin E itself. It has a yellowish color and is soluble both in water and in oil. Vitamin E has a skin smoothing, cell-renewing, and anti-inflammatory effect and is especially well suited for wound healing.

Wheat Germ Oil, Bran Absolute

INCI: *Triticum Vulgare* (Wheat) Germ Oil

Wheat germ oil helps strengthen and firm the connective tissue. Besides moisturizing and nourishing the skin, it promotes skin health by improving blood circulation, which can delay the signs of premature skin aging. Especially important for dry and wrinkle-prone mature skin are its regenerative properties and ability to positively influence cell growth. Wheat germ oil is equally well suited for regular maintenance of normal hair and the treatment of insufficient subcutaneous scalp blood flow.

Wheat germ oil is a very good base carrier for essential oils. It can be used in a variety of products, such as powders, skin oils, soaps, face packs, and more. Rich in tocopherol, this oil is a natural source of vitamin E and unsaturated fatty acids. Wheat germ oil will keep for approximately 6 months, provided it is stored cool and protected from light.

Xanthan Gum

INCI: Xanthan Gum

Xanthan gum is used in cosmetics to prepare clear acqueous gels. It functions as a stabilizer for emulsions with low emulsifier concentrations and reliably thickens formulations containing tensides.

Xanthan gum is completely irritant-free since its large molecules prevent it from penetrating into the skin's horny layer. Because it is temperature-sensitive, it should never be heated to more than 70°C (158°F). Unlike regular xanthan, xanthan gum gets absorbed into the skin nearly residue-free and is also much easier to process. Xanthan gels are pH-stable (pH 4 to 11), are compatible with applications containing a certain amount of salt, and remain stable under a wide range of temperatures. The recommended use level is around 0.2 percent.

Xanthan gum can be mixed directly into the cold or warm water phase. If you want to take no chances with possible lumping, presoak it in a small amount of 70 vol% alcohol or glycerin, then add this predissolved mixture to the water phase, stirring continuously.

Xanthan gels are shear thinning, meaning their viscosity decreases with higher shear rates because their cross-linked molecule structure gets destroyed so they thin out. When creating a high-viscosity gel formulation, you should therefore avoid overly vigorous agitation (such as stirring with an immersion blender).

Xyliance

INCI: Cetearyl Wheat Straw Glycosides (and) Cetearyl Alcohol

Xyliance is an oil-in-water emulsifier approved for use in natural cosmetics. It is very pH stable and therefore easily processable. When added to creams, it creates light, nongreasy formulations that leave a silky feel on the skin. Recommended use levels are from 2 to 5 percent in proportion to the total weight of all ingredients. Xyliance is best used for creams containing a lipid phase (from 20 to 25 percent). The ideal phase temperature is 70°C (158°F).

Zinc Oxide

INCI: Zinc Oxide

Zinc oxide, the oxidized metal zinc, is known as the pigment zinc white. Because of its anti-inflammatory and drying effect, it is often used as additive for powder (at a level of 5 to 10 percent).

Facial Cleansers

Facial skin is regarded as highly sensitive. On this account, it needs special treatment, starting with regular cleansing. Whether you have more oily or rather dry skin will determine the best ratio between lipid-replenishing substances and nurturing ingredients tailored to the unique needs of your personal skin type. Individual age, too, is important to consider when choosing which ingredients would be most beneficial. Last but not least come your personal preferences regarding consistency, scent, and color of your cosmetic products. Choose between whipped cleansing cream or regular washing cream, cleansing milk, peel, or facial toner. Get carried away by the scent of wild rose, lemon, calendula, coconut, or vanilla. Try this and that to find out which ingredient will act as a pick-me-up in the morning, and what will feel soothing to round off the day.

Argan & Wild Rose Creamy Face Wash

For sensitive and aging skin

Ingredients

Phase A (lipid phase)

1.5 g (0.053 oz) glyceryl stearate SE

2.5 g (0.088 oz) Xyliance

1 g (0.035 oz) Avocadin®

9 g (0.317 oz) argan oil

2 g (0.071 oz) shea butter

Phase B (water phase)

68 g (0.282 oz) rose hydrolate

8 g (0.282 oz) glycerin

0.1 g (0.035 oz) xanthan gum

4 g (0.141 oz) Rüger healing chalk

1 g (0.035 oz) Facetensid HT

2 g (0.071 oz) silk powder

Phase C

2 g (0.071 oz) oat extract

2 g (0.071 oz) wild rose oil (or rosehip kernel oil)

6 drops attar of rose (or 2 drops rose essential and 4 drops sandalwood oil)

20 drops Paraben K

2 drops citric acid

1 Place the emulsifiers glyceryl stearate SE and Xyliance into a beaker together with the Avocadin® and the argan oil and heat this mixture to 75°C (167°F). Once everything has melted clear, remove from heat and add in shea butter. Shea butter will continue to melt without further heating (photo 1).

2 Meanwhile, place rose hydrolate and glycerin into a second beaker and heat this mixture to 75°C (167°F) too. Switch off the burner and fold in xanthan to form a gel (photo 2). Then, carefully add healing chalk, Facetensid HT, and silk powder. Stir this mass to a homogeneous consistency (photo 3).

3 Now, add the water phase into the lipid phase (photo 4) and mix both at medium speed for 3 to 5 minutes, then continue stirring with a spatula until the emulsion has cooled to about 35°C (95°F) (photo 5).

4 Finally, fold in oat extract, wild rose oil, essential oils, Paraben K, and citric acid to complete your cleansing cream formulation (photo 6).

5 When the full recommended 20 drops of Paraben K have been used, this cleansing cream can be kept for approximately 6 months. With only 10 drops Paraben K added, shelf life will be reduced to 3 months.

Tip: Fill cleansing cream into a pump dispenser and apply a hazelnut-sized dab to your dry face in the morning and evening. Foam up using a small amount of water and rinse with plenty of water afterward.

Tea Tree & Lemon Facial Cleansing Cream

Ingredients

Phase A

2 g (0.071 oz) thyme extract

0.1 g (0.003 oz) xanthan gum

Phase B (lipid phase)

4 g (0.141 oz) glyceryl stearate SE

8 g (0.282 oz) safflower oil

4 g (0.141 oz) hemp oil

3 g (0.106 oz) babassu oil

Phase C (water phase)

8 g (0.282 oz) glycerin

30 g (1.06 oz) tea tree hydrolate

30 g (1.06 oz) witch hazel hydrolate

3 g (0.106 oz) ghassoul (lava clay)

2 g (0.071 oz) Dead Sea mud

1.5 g (0.053 oz) sucrose cocoate

Phase D

2 g (0.071 oz) algae gel

12 drops essential oils (5 drops tea tree, 2 drops manuka, 1 drop cajeput, 4 drops lemon)

10–20 drops Paraben K

1 First, mix the thyme extract with the xanthan. Then, put the emulgator glyceryl stearate SE, safflower oil, hemp oil, and the babassu oil into a second beaker and heat to 75°C (167°F). Once everything has melted clear, remove the beaker from the burner.

2 Meanwhile, heat the glycerin together with the tea tree and witch hazel hydrolates to 75°C (167°F), too. Remove the beaker from the heat source and stir in the ghassoul, Dead Sea mud, and sucrose cocoate until you've created a homogeneous mixture. This is best done with an immersion blender. Stir in thyme extract/xanthan and mix everything well.

3 Now, add the water phase into the lipid phase and, using a kitchen mixer or immersion blender, slowly stir both together on medium speed for 3 to 5 minutes, until the emulsion has turned stable. Now, continue stirring with a glass stirrer until the mixture has cooled to 35°C (95°F).

4 Finally, add in algae gel and, at the very end, the essential oils and Paraben K.

Tip: **Tea Tree & Lemon Facial Cleansing Cream can be applied the same way as Argan & Wild Rose Creamy Face Wash and is also suitable for use with a pump dispenser.**

Facial Cleansing Cream

For normal skin

Ingredients

Phase A

80 g (2.82 fl oz) neroli hydrolate

Phase B

25 g (0.882 oz) almond bran

4.4 g (0.155 oz) almond meal

3 g (0.106 oz) almond milk powder

Phase C

4 g (0.141 oz) calendula extract (alcohol 70 vol%)

4 g (0.141 oz) St. John's wort extract (alcohol 70 vol%)

4 g (0.141 oz) witch hazel extract (alcohol 70 vol%)

4 g (0.141 oz) German chamomile extract (alcohol 70 vol%)

0.1 g (0.035 oz) xanthan gum

Phase D

6 g (0.212 oz) almond oil (vanilla-macerate)

5 g (0.176 oz) wheat germ oil

10.5 g (0.370 oz) prune kernel oil

30 drops Paraben K or Phenonip

1 First, put the neroli hydrolate in a beaker and bring to a short boil to kill off any possible germs. Then, using a separate vessel, mix Phase B ingredients (almond bran, almond meal, and almond milk powder).

2 Next, place all of the alcoholic extracts in a beaker, then stir in xanthan. When the hydrolate has cooled, add the Paraben K. Add this mixture to the almond bran and stir until it has formed a homogeneous paste.

3 Finally, weigh out the oils and mix everything together thoroughly. Wait for 2 to 3 hours before putting the paste in cosmetic containers or tubes; it happens fairly often that the almond bran continues to set, thickening the paste too much. Should this happen, simply add a few milliliters hydrolate and extract [at a rate of 8.7 g (0.247 oz) hydrolate to 1.3 g alcoholic extract 75 vol%], until the mixture has the consistency of a creamy puree.

Tips: You can substitute the almond bran, almond meal, and almond milk powder with just almond bran alone.

Alcoholic extracts preserve your Facial Cleansing Cream, prolonging its shelf life. Regrettably, more and more commercially available extracts are extracts in propylene glycol, which has weaker preserving properties.

Cleansing Milk

For combination skin

Ingredients

Phase A

2 g (0.071 oz) green tea extract

1.5 g (0.053 oz) cucumber extract

1.5 g (0.053 oz) witch hazel extract

14 g (0.494 oz) nettle extract (alcoholic)

0.1 g (0.003 oz) xanthan gum

Phase B (lipid phase)

5 g (0.176 oz) glyceryl stearate

5 g (0.176 oz) emulsan

1 g (0.035 oz) Avocadin®

5 g (0.176 oz) jojoba oil

5 g (0.176 oz) avocado oil

14 g (0.494 oz) virgin soy oil

5 g (0.176 oz) broccoli seed oil

10 g (0.353 oz) safflower oil

3 g (0.106 oz) sucrose cocoate

2.5 g (0.088 oz) fluid lecithin CM

Phase C (water phase)

86 g (3.034 oz) witch hazel hydrolate

1 Combine all extracts in a beaker and add in xanthan while stirring.

2 Melt emulsifiers glyceryl stearate and emulsan together with Avocadin® and jojoba oil until the mixture becomes clear. Add in remaining oils, sucrose cocoate, and fluid lecithin CM, then heat this mixture to 75°C (167°F).

3 Heat witch hazel hydrolate to 75°C (167°F) too. When both phases have reached a temperature of 75°C (167°F), add the water phase into the lipid phase. Stir both with an immersion blender on high speed. When a stable emulsion has formed, continue stirring with a glass stirrer.

4 When the cleansing milk has cooled down slightly, add the extract/xanthan mixture. Continue stirring with a glass stirrer until the cleansing milk has completely cooled.

5 Preserved with alcohol, the cleansing milk will keep for 10 to 12 weeks.

Tip: Decant the cleansing milk into a pump dispenser. To clean your face, place a hazelnut-sized dab into your palm and apply to the moistened face. Rinse with lukewarm water.

Coconut-Almond Creamy Face Wash

For normal skin

Ingredients

Phase A (lipid phase)

4 g (0.141 oz) almond oil

8 g (0.282 oz) virgin coconut oil

4 g (0.141 oz) glyceryl stearate SE

Phase B

0.5 g (0.018 oz) Plantapon® SF

0.1 g (0.003 oz) Lamesoft®

4 g (0.141 oz) kaolin (white lava clay)

Phase C (water phase)

40 g (1.411 oz) water

35 g (1.234 oz) coconut cream

Phase D

10 g (0.353 oz) glycerin

0.1 g (0.003 oz) xanthan gum

1–2 drops lactic or citric acid (for a pH of 5.5)

0.5–0.8 g (0.018–0.028 oz) Phenonip (liquid parabens)

2–4 drops bitter almond oil

1

2

3   4   5

1   Heat almond oil, coconut oil, and the emulgator glyceryl stearate SE in a beaker to 75°C (167°F), until the glyceryl stearate SE has completely melted. Heat the water and the coconut cream to 75°C (167°F) too.

2   Carefully stir surfactants Plantapon® SF and Lamesoft® into the lipid phase, taking care to avoid frothing. Add in kaolin and continue stirring until a homogeneous mixture has formed (photo 1).

3   Place the glycerin into a second beaker and pour the xanthan in under constant stirring to avoid lumping (photo 2).

4   When both lipid phase and water phase have reached exactly 75°C (167°F), slowly add the water phase into the lipid phase. Using an electric milk frother or immersion blender on high speed, stir for 2 to 3 minutes, until the emulsion has turned stable (photo 3). Then, continue stirring the mixture with a glass stirrer until it has cooled down to approximately 40°C (104°F).

5   Now, carefully stir the xanthan-thickened glycerin into the emulsion, thoroughly combining all of the ingredients (photo 4). After the lotion has completely cooled, measure its pH and adjust when necessary. To preserve, add Phenonip (photo 5). Finally, add bitter almond oil until the desired fragrance intensity has been reached.

6   Because of the coconut cream contained within, this cleansing cream should be stored in a cool, dark place and used up as quickly as possible.

Tips: Because of its viscosity, this cleansing cream is best stored in a cosmetics jar, but if desired, it could potentially be kept in a pump dispenser as well.

If you wish to preserve your cleansing cream using potassium sorbate solution, its pH should not be more than 5.5. I recommend using Phenonip for preservation instead, since coconut cream is very susceptible to germ infestation.

Mild Facial Peel

For all skin types

Ingredients

Phase A

1 g (0.003 oz) virgin coconut oil

2 g (0.071 oz) apricot kernel oil

2 g (0.071 oz) almond oil

50 g (1.763 oz) Facetensid HT

10 g (0.353 oz) Plantapon® SF

5 g (0.176 oz) sucrose cocoate

5 g (0.176 oz) fluid lecithin CM

Phase B

148 g (0.282 oz) rose hydrolate or boiled water

2 g (0.071 oz) silk protein

2 g (0.071 oz) Optiphen

Phase C

16 g (0.212 oz) Rewoderm®

Phase D

5 g (0.176 oz) jojoba beads (red or blue)

2 g (0.071 oz) essential oil blend [1 g (0.035 oz) grapefruit, 0.5 g (0.018 oz) green tangerine, 0.5 g (0.018 oz) limette]

1 First, melt the coconut oil in a beaker. Add apricot and almond oils, then the remaining Phase A ingredients, and mix thoroughly by stirring (photo 1). In a second large beaker, mix the hydrolate with the silk protein and the preservatives. Then, carefully pour Phase A into this mixture and stir, using a spatula or electric mixer, until all ingredients have combined well (photo 2). You have created a low-viscosity liquid (photo 3).

2 There are different options for thickening a liquid. While xanthan is used for a number of formulations, this recipe uses Rewoderm® as thickener. Rewoderm® is a surfactant which, when added to a recipe, will cause the surfactant blend to thicken. You can add Rewoderm® until your preparation has reached the perfect consistency (photo 4)—just keep in mind that it will take a while until the final consistency has been achieved. I find an amount of 16 g (0.212 oz) optimal. If you want, you can add 18 to 20 g (0.635 to 0.705 oz) without worrying.

3 Finally, add the jojoba beads (photo 5) and the fragrance blend, stir, and pour the preparation into a bottle. This facial peel should be used up within 4 weeks.

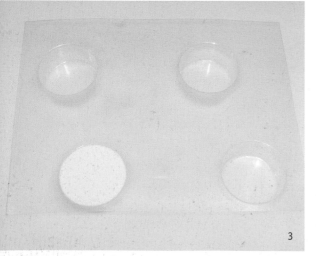

Vanilla Cleansing Bar (25% fat)

For normal skin

Ingredients

Phase A

68 g (2.4 oz) SLSA powder

4 g (0.141 oz) silk powder

2 g (0.071 oz) powdered
pearl

Phase B (lipid phase)

3 g (0.106 oz) rice bran oil

4 g (0.141 oz) camellia seed
oil

13 g (0.459 oz) shea butter

5 g (0.176 oz) mango butter

½ vanilla pod

8 drops vanilla extract

1 Wearing a protective face mask to avoid inhaling particle matter, place SLSA powder, silk powder, and pearl powder into a bowl and combine well.

2 Put rice bran oil, camellia seed oil, shea butter, and mango butter in a beaker and melt in a water bath at low temperature. Add vanilla bean along with pulp and let the mixture steep. After approximately 20 minutes, remove the vanilla bean. Take the beaker out of the water bath.

3 Stir in the vanilla extract and add the lipid phase to the bowl containing the dry ingredients (photo 1). Mix everything thoroughly (photo 2), then press the mixture in molds (photo 3). Place the filled molds in the freezer for about 1 hour. After this freezer treatment, the cleansing bars can be easily released from their molds.

Tip: Silicone molds are unsuitable for casting cleansing bars because the silicone will give too much when being filled. Better suited are soap dies and plastic molds, available in many pretty designs from any well-stocked soap-making supply shop.

Cleansing Bar with Sea-Buckthorn and Healing Chalk (40% fat)

For dry and mature skin

Ingredients

Phase A

55 g (1.940 oz) SLSA powder

5 g (0.176 oz) Rüger healing chalk

Phase B (lipid phase)

5.5 g (0.194 oz) almond oil

4.5 g (0.159 oz) sea-buckthorn seed oil

25 g (0.882 oz) shea butter

4 g (0.141 oz) D-panthenol

0.5 g (0.018 oz) orange essential oil

0.5 g (0.018 oz) sea-buckthorn berry oil

1 Wearing a protective face mask to avoid inhaling fine particle dust, mix SLSA powder and healing chalk in a bowl.

2 Place almond oil, sea-buckthorn seed oil, and shea butter in a beaker and melt in a water bath at low temperature. Remove the beaker from the water bath and let the mixture cool to 35°C (95°F). Now, add D-panthenol and orange oil.

3 Add the lipid phase to the dry ingredients in the bowl and combine everything thoroughly to create a homogeneous dough. Knead in the sea-buckthorn berry oil to color your dough orange.

4 Fill the dough in molds, pressing as firmly as possible to create relief patterns.

5 Put the filled molds in the freezer for about 1 hour. Now your cleansing bars can be easily removed from their molds.

Milk & Honey Cleansing Bar (43% fat)

For sensitive skin

Ingredients

Phase A

20 g (0.705 oz) mare's milk powder (or other milk powder)

30 g (1.06 oz) SLSA powder

7 g (0.247 oz) honey powder

Phase B (lipid phase)

1 g (0.035 oz) Avocadin®

7 g (0.247 oz) almond oil

20 g (0.705 oz) cocoa butter

15 g (0.529 oz) shea butter

10–15 drops honey absolute or honey aroma

1 Wearing a protective face mask to avoid inhaling fine particle dust, combine milk powder and SLSA powder in a bowl.

2 Put Avocadin® and almond oil in a beaker and let both melt in a water bath. After the Avocadin® has melted clear, switch off the burner, but let the beaker remain in the water bath.

3 Add in the cocoa butter and the shea butter, mixing with a glass stirrer until everything has melted. If necessary, turn the burner back on; however, the lipid phase must not become too hot or the cocoa butter and shea butter will turn grainy. Let the lipid phase cool down to 35°C (95°F) before stirring in the honey powder and honey absolute.

4 Now, add the lipid phase to the dry ingredients and knead them together thoroughly.
   This is best done by hand (don't forget to wear gloves). Press the mixture into molds and refrigerate for about 1 hour before releasing.

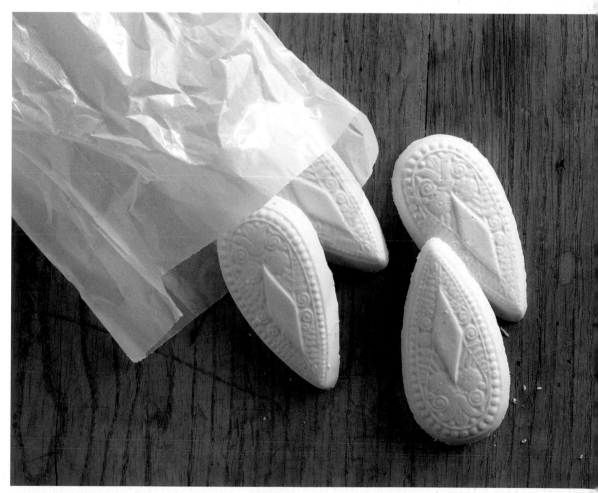

Facial Toners for All Skin Types

For Blemished Skin

Ingredients

50 g (1.763 oz) witch hazel hydrolate

30 g (1.06 oz) German chamomile hydrolate

14 g (0.494 oz) nettle extract or witch hazel extract (alcohol 70 vol%)

3 g (0.106 oz) cucumber extract

2.9 g (0.102 oz) green tea extract

0.1 g (0.003 oz) vitamin C (ascorbic acid)

1 Mix all ingredients well and decant the facial toner into a spray bottle.

2 Preserved with alcohol, the facial toner can be kept for about 10 weeks.

For Dry Skin

Ingredients

40 g (1.411 oz) pure aloe vera

41 g (0.035 oz) *Jasminum sambac* hydrolate

8.5 g (0.300 oz) ethanol (95 vol%)

0.1 g (0.035 oz) allantoin

0.4 g (0.014 oz) wheat protein (elastin)

2 g (0.071 oz) silk protein

6 g (0.212 oz) cucumber extract

3 g (0.106 oz) jujube (da zao) extract

2 g (0.071 oz) Lipodermin

1 Combine pure aloe vera, *Jasminum sambac* hydrolate, and ethanol and pour into a spray bottle. Add remaining ingredients and shake vigorously until allantoin, wheat protein, and Lipodermin have completely dissolved.

2 Stored cool and dark, this facial toner will keep for approximately 6 weeks.

For Aging Skin

Ingredients

11.5 g (0.053 oz) green tea extract (alcohol 70 vol%) *or* 8.5 g (0.300 oz) ethanol (95 vol%)

0.1 g (0.003 oz) hyaluronic acid

80 g (2.82 fl oz) rose hydrolate

2 g (0.071 oz) silk protein

0.1 g (0.003 oz) vitamin C (ascorbic acid)

4.3 g (0.152 oz) honey

2 g (0.071 oz) glycerin

1 Put green tea extract *or* ethanol into a beaker and stir in hyaluronic acid.

2 Place the remaining ingredients into a second beaker and stir until the honey and vitamin C have completely dissolved. Under continuous stirring, pour in the extract blend. Any possible lumps will dissolve within a few hours. Put the facial toner in a spray bottle.

3 Stored cool and dark, the facial toner will keep for approximately 4 to 6 weeks.

Tip: Morning and evening after cleansing, spray facial toner onto skin and gently pat in.

Facial Care Products

Just as with facial cleansing products, other products for facial care should be tailored to your skin type. Depending on your individual needs, recommended care products should contain particular skin care substances and be more or less rich in fats and oils. Ultimately, you will have to try out various options before deciding which types of products suit you best. Of course, modifications of the recipes introduced here are always encouraged! In addition to facial creams based on shea and mango butter or such exotic oils as jojoba, argan, babassu, and papaya, this chapter will delight you with Hydrating Eye Gel and Blackberry Lip Gloss—sounds enticing, doesn't it?

1

3

4

Hydrating Eye Gel with Pearl Extract

For dry skin

Ingredients

Phase A

20 g (0.705 oz) neroli hydrolate

2.5 g (0.088 oz) urea

1 g (0.035 oz) D-panthenol

1 g (0.035 oz) vitamin E acetate

1.8 g (0.063 oz) cucumber extract

Phase B

5.5 g (0.194 oz) ethanol

0.7 g (0.025 oz) xanthan gum

Phase C

17 g (0.600 oz) cornflower hydrolate

0.1 g (0.003 oz) hyaluronic acid

0.1 g (0.003 oz) aloe vera, 10:1

Phase D

6 drops neroli essential oil

0.5 g (0.018 oz) pink-colored beads of pearl extract

10 drops potassium sorbate solution, 5:1

1 drop lactic acid (for a pH of 5.5)

1 Fill neroli hydrolate into a beaker, then add urea under constant stirring until it has completely dissolved. Now, dissolve D-panthenol, vitamin E acetate, and cucumber extract in the solution the same way (photo 1).

2 Place ethanol in a second large beaker and add xanthan while stirring. Put cornflower hydrolate in a third beaker and stir in hyaluronic acid and aloe vera.

3 Using an immersion blender, stir Phase A into Phase B for approximately 30 seconds (photo 2), then continue stirring with a spatula until a clear gel has formed. Now, mix Phase C into the gel (photo 3). Finally, carefully stir essential neroli oil, pink beads, potassium sorbate solution, and lactic acid into the gel (photo 4).

Blackberry Lip Gloss

Ingredients

0.6 g (0.021 oz) Ceralan™

0.6 g (0.021 oz) Olivem®

1.4 g (0.049 oz) jojoba oil

5.3 g (0.187 oz) phytolanolin

3.3 g (0.116 oz) castor oil

3.5 g (0.123 oz) ultramarine rose pigment or pink-colored lava clay

1.2 g (0.042 oz) titanium dioxide

1.2 g (0.042 oz) Silk White

0.6 g (0.021 oz) vitamin E

2 drops blackberry food flavoring

1 Place Ceralan™, Olivem®, jojoba oil, phytolanolin, and castor oil into a beaker (photo 1) and melt everything in a water bath until the mixture has turned clear.

2 Using a glass stirrer, stir in the pigments until the mixture has cooled to 35°C (95°F) (photo 2). Now, add vitamin E and food flavoring. Finally, pour the lip gloss into a tube (photo 3).

Tip: Try replacing the phytolanolin with lanolin or enhancing the scent by adding organic-grade lemon or orange essential oil with a pinch of Stevia powder. You can experiment with color too—use the luster pigment mica violet for darker hues.

1

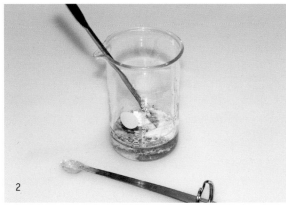

2

3

Currant Cream

For dry skin

Ingredients

Phase A (water phase)

44 g (1.552 oz) currant hydrolate

Phase B

5 g (0.176 oz) ethanol

0.2 g (0.007 oz) xanthan gum

Phase C (lipid phase)

2 g (0.071 oz) emulsan

3 g (0.106 oz) glyceryl stearate

2 g (0.071 oz) Avocadin®

8 g (0.282 oz) jojoba oil

5 g (0.176 oz) almond oil

7 g (0.247 oz) shea butter

Phase D

10 g (0.353 oz) currant hydrolate

2 g (0.071 oz) sodium lactate

2 g (0.071 oz) silk protein

3 g (0.106 oz) urea

Phase E

3 g (0.106 oz) black currant seed oil

1 g (0.035 oz) tocopherol

1 g (0.035 oz) vitamin E acetate

2 drops lactic acid

2 drops rose oil

10–20 drops Paraben K or 18 drops potassium sorbate solution (5:1) [equals 0.2 g (0.007 oz) potassium sorbate granules]

1

2

3

1 Place the 44 g (1.552 oz) of currant hydrolate into a beaker and heat to 75°C (167°F).

2 Put emulsifiers emulsan and glyceryl stearate into a second beaker, together with Avocadin®, jojoba oil, and almond oil. Melt the oils until clear, then heat them to 75°C (167°F) too. Add shea butter and wait until it has melted.

3 In the remaining 10 g (0.353 oz) of currant hydrolate, dissolve sodium lactate, silk protein, and urea.

4 In yet another beaker, dissolve the xanthan in ethanol.

5 When the oil and water phases have reached exactly the same temperature [between 70 and 75°C (158 and 167°F)], remove the beakers from the burner and stir the ethanol/xanthan blend into the water phase until it has reached a gel-like consistency.

6 Using an immersion blender on high speed, gradually stir this mixture into the lipid phase (photo 1). After approximately 5 minutes, a stable emulsion will have formed (photo 2). Now, continue stirring with a glass stirrer or spatula until the cream has cooled to 35°C (95°F).

7 Under constant stirring, gradually add in the currant hydrolate, sodium lactate, silk protein, and urea. Then, drop by drop, add the black currant seed oil, tocopherol, vitamin E acetate, and rose oil (photo 3).

8 Test the cream's pH and, if necessary, adjust it by adding 1 to 2 drops of lactic acid. If you want to preserve your cream with potassium sorbate solution, its pH should be at 5 to 5.4. Work in 18 drops of potassium sorbate solution. When preserving with Paraben K, the pH is not crucial.

9 When preserved with potassium sorbate solution, this cream will keep for about 6 weeks. Preserved with 10 to 20 drops of Paraben K, the cream can be kept for approximately 3 to 6 months.

Tip: The pH is best measured using pH indicator strips with four testing panels. It will take about 3 to 5 minutes for the indicator to show its final coloration.

Jasmine Hydrating Gel

For dehydrated, mature skin

Ingredients

Phase A

40 g (1.411 oz) *Jasminum sambac* hydrolate

4 g (0.141 oz) glycerin

3 g (0.106 oz) silk protein

2.8 g (0.099 oz) Lipodermin

Optional: 1 pinch grape extract

4 g (0.141 oz) Natural Moisturizing Factor NMF

Phase B

30 g (1.06 oz) jasmine extract (alcohol 70 vol%)

0.8 g (0.028 oz) xanthan gum

0.2 g (0.007 oz) hyaluronic acid

Phase C

4 g (0.141 oz) cactus pear seed oil

4 g (0.141 oz) argan oil

6 g (0.212 oz) jojoba oil

1 g (0.035 oz) vitamin E acetate

5 drops sandalwood essential oil

2 drops ylang ylang essential oil

1 First, combine all of the Phase A ingredients. Pour jasmine extract into a large beaker, then disperse xanthan and hyaluronic acid in it. Mix Phase C ingredients.

2 Add Phase A to Phase B and mix both of them until a gel has formed. Then, drop by drop, stir in Phase C until the mixture is homogenous. Finally, pour the hydrating gel into a pump dispenser.

3 The hydrating gel can be kept for 4 to 6 weeks.

Hydro-Lipid Shake Lotion for Mature Skin

Ingredients

Phase A (water phase)

42 g (1.482 oz) rose hydrolate

1.25 g (0.044 oz) glycerin

4 g (0.141 oz) silk protein

0.1 g (0.003 oz) grape extract (or beet root extract)

1.25 g (0.044 oz) urea

0.2 g (0.007 oz) sodium lactate

1 drop lactic acid

0.1 g (0.003 oz) aloe vera powder, 10:1

0.1 g (0.003 oz) hyaluronic acid

6.5 g (0.229 oz) ethanol (95 vol%)

Phase B (lipid phase)

20 g (0.705 oz) wheat germ oil

12 g (0.423 oz) argan oil

10 g (0.353 oz) squalane

3.4 g (0.120 oz) wild rose oil

3 g (0.106 oz) evening primrose oil

0.5 g (0.018 oz) vitamin E

0.5 g (0.018 oz) vitamin E acetate

0.5 g (0.018 oz) wild rose CO_2 extract

0.1 g (0.003 oz) essential oil blend (1 drop rose and 2 drops sandalwood)

1 Pour rose hydrolate into a beaker. Stir in glycerin, silk protein, and grape extract. Add urea and stir until everything has dissolved. Now, add sodium lactate and lactic acid und stir until they, too, have dissolved.

2 Using an electric milk frother or immersion blender, stir aloe vera powder and hyaluronic acid into ethanol for about 1 minute. Then carefully combine this mixture with the water phase.

3 Gradually combine all ingredients for the lipid phase. Finally, decant into a bottle—first the water phase, followed by the lipid phase. Shake bottle before every use to recombine the phases.

4 Stored cool and dry, Hydro-Lipid Shake Lotion will keep for 4 to 6 weeks.

Tip: Urea will dissolve slowly in cold rose hydrolate. To speed up the process, the urea may be pulverized using a mortar and pestel before processing.

Tea Tree Cream

For blemished skin

Ingredients

Phase A (water phase)

20 g (0.705 oz) tea tree hydrolate

10.5 g (0.370 oz) myrtle hydrolate

Phase B (lipid phase)

2 g (0.071 oz) safflower oil

2 g (0.071 oz) grape seed oil

4.5 g (0.159 oz) babassu oil

1.5 g (0.053 oz) squalane

1 g (0.035 oz) cetyl alcohol

2 g (0.071 oz) Xyliance

Phase C

6.5 g (0.229 oz) neem extract

0.1 g (0.003 oz) xanthan gum

Phase D

1 g (0.035 oz) vitamin E acetate

1 g (0.035 oz) sodium PCA

11 drops essential oils (2 drops tea tree,
    2 drops manuka, 7 drops lemon)

5–10 drops Paraben K

1 In a beaker, heat tea tree and myrtle hydrolates to 75°C (167°F). Place all Phase B ingredients into a second beaker and heat to 75°C (167°F) too.

2 Meanwhile, put neem extract into a small beaker and stir in the xanthan.

3 When both the water phase and the lipid phase have reached a temperature of 75°C (167°F), use a milk frother or an immersion blender to stir the neem extract/xanthan blend into the water phase, creating a low viscosity gel.

4 Under constant stirring, slowly add the gel to the lipid phase, then mix on high speed for approximately 1 to 2 minutes, until the emulsion has turned stable. Now, continue stirring with a glass stirrer until the mixture has cooled to 35°C (95°F). Work in Phase D ingredients drop by drop.
    Put the Tea Tree Cream into a cosmetic container, tube, or airless dispenser.

5 Preserved with 5 drops of Paraben K, this cream will keep for 3 months; with 10 drops of Paraben K, 6 months.

Facial Cream with Camellia and Papaya Oil

For normal and combination skin

Ingredients

Phase A (water phase)

30 g (1.06 oz) neroli hydrolate

1 g (0.035 oz) glycerin

Phase B (lipid phase)

2.6 g (0.212 oz) glyceryl stearate SE

0.5 g (0.018 oz) cetyl alcohol

2 g (0.071 oz) babassu oil

4 g (0.141 oz) camellia seed oil

2 g (0.071 oz) shea butter

2 g (0.071 oz) papaya oil

Phase C

3 g (0.106 oz) ethanol

0.1 g (0.003 oz) xanthan gum

Phase D

1 g (0.035 oz) D-panthenol

1 g (0.035 oz) silk protein

1 drop lactic acid

2 drops ylang ylang essential oil

2 drops green tangerine essential oil

2 drops neroli essential oil

5–10 drops Paraben K or 0.25–0.75 g (0.009–0.026 oz) Optiphen

1 In a beaker, heat neroli hydrolate and glycerin in a water bath to 75°C (167°F). Place glyceryl stearate SE, cetyl alcohol, babassu oil, and camellia seed oil into a second beaker and heat in water bath to 75°C (167°F) too.

2 Switch off the burner. Keep both beakers in the water bath. Add shea butter and papaya oil into the lipid phase.

3 Meanwhile, add xanthan to ethanol and stir both into the water phase.

4 When the shea butter has completely melted, add the water phase under constant stirring into the lipid phase. Stir the mixture on high speed for 1 to 2 minutes until it is homogenous. Continue stirring with a glass stirrer or spatula until the cream has cooled to 35°C (95°F). If you prefer, you may place the beaker in a cold water bath.

5 Drop by drop, add the ethanol/xanthan mixture and combine everything well. Finally, gradually add in Phase D ingredients. Preserve your facial cream with Paraben K or Optiphen.

6 When preserved with 5 to 10 drops Paraben K, this facial cream will keep for 3 to 6 months.

Mare's Milk Cream

For dry skin

Ingredients

Phase A (water phase)

40 g (1.411 oz) mare's milk

16 g (0.564 oz) aloe vera

5 g (0.176 oz) glycerin

0.1 g (0.003 oz) xanthan gum

Phase B (lipid phase)

2.5 g (0.088 oz) emulsan

2.5 g (0.088 oz) glyceryl stearate

1 g (0.035 oz) candelilla wax

10 g (0.353 oz) jojoba oil

13 g (0.459 oz) shea butter

5 g (0.176 oz) mango butter

Phase C

2.5 g (0.088 oz) evening primrose oil

1.5 g (0.053 oz) wild rose oil

1 g (0.035 oz) D-panthenol

20 drops Paraben K or Phenonip (liquid parabens)

1 Place mare's milk and aloe vera into a beaker and heat the mixture in a water bath to 75°C (167°F). Dissolve the xanthan in the glycerin and stir it into the hot water phase. Put emulsan, glyceryl stearate, candelilla wax, and jojoba oil into a second beaker and heat these ingredients in a water bath to 75°C (167°F) too.

2 Turn off the burner. Keep the beakers in the water bath. Add shea butter and mango butter into the lipid phase and stir until both have completely melted.

3 Gradually add the water phase into the lipid phase and mix on high speed for approximately 2 minutes, until a stable emulsion has formed. Now, continue stirring with a spatula until the cream has cooled to 35°C (95°F). Drop by drop, add Phase C ingredients and fold into the cream.

4 Filled in a jar and stored cool, this cream will keep for approximately 8 weeks.

German Chamomile & Honey Cream

For dry skin

Ingredients

Phase A (lipid phase)

6.5 g (0.229 oz) Olivem®

1.5 g (0.053 oz) Avocadin®

9.5 g (0.335 oz) shea butter

10 g (0.353 oz) olive oil

4 g (0.141 oz) squalane

3 g (0.106 oz) candelilla wax

Phase B (water phase)

41.9 g (1.48 oz) German chamomile hydrolate

Phase C

5.5 g (0.194 oz) hemp oil

5 g (0.176 oz) evening primrose oil

5 g (0.176 oz) avocado oil

Phase D

6.9 g (0.243 oz) German chamomile tincture (75 vol%)

0.1 g (0.003 oz) aloe vera, 200:1

0.1 g (0.003 oz) xanthan gum

1 g (0.035 oz) non-water-soluble silk or kaolin (white lava clay)

10 drops essential oils (3 drops Roman chamomile, 4 drops honey, 3 drops vanilla)

1 Measure all Phase A ingredients into a beaker and heat on a burner to 80°C (176°F). In a second beaker, heat the German chamomile hydrolate to 80°C (176°F), too.

2 Meanwhile, in a third beaker, stir aloe vera and xanthan into German chamomile tincture.

3 When the lipid phase and the water phase both have reached an identical temperature of 80°C (176°F), drop by drop stir the lipid phase into the water phase, using a spatula or a glass stirrer.

Please note: The water-in-oil emulsion should not be agitated on high with a mixer or immersion blender. To prevent the emulsion from cooling down too quickly, refrain from using a water bath to cool.

4 When the emulsion has cooled to 35 to 40°C (95 to 104°F), stir in the oils from Phase C.
Now, add the German chamomile tincture with aloe vera and xanthan. Finally, stir the water-insoluble silk and the essential oils into the cream. This cream has a high fat content (50%). Stir until completely cooled.

5 The cream should be used within approximately 8 weeks.

Body Cleansers

Thorough cleansing is the prerequisite for effective skin care. However, the cleansing process can also turn into a sensuous experience on its own, courtesy of this chapter's bath bars, shower smoothies, Red Rose Peeling Oil, and Rose & Vanilla Bathing Oil—guaranteed! Your hair will be taken care of as well: Choose between practical Tea Tree Shampoo or uncover the mysterious Cleopatra's Secret. If you have children, be prepared to be pestered about sharing your delightfully wobbly shower jellies or yummy strawberry shower gel with glitter. Better lock the bathroom door to indulge in your frothy delight!

Chocolate & Vanilla Bath Bars

For all skin types

Ingredients

For 2 Bath Bars

100 g (3.527 oz) cocoa butter

40 g (1.411 oz) shea butter

50 g (1.764 oz) milk powder

6 g (0.212 oz) lysolecithin

Additionally, for Vanilla-Scented Bar

1 vanilla pod

2 g (0.071 oz) vanilla bean perfume oil

Additionally, for Chocolate-Scented Bar

1 tsp cocoa powder

2 g (0.071 oz) chocolate perfume oil

1 Melt cocoa butter and shea butter in a beaker on low heat in a water bath. Taking care not to let the fats get too hot will retain the ingredients' nourishing properties and also help the bars solidify with a neat appearance.

2 Switch off burner and add milk powder and lysolecithin to the fats. Mix with an immersion blender until homogeneous, then divide the mixture in two equal portions.

3 To half of the mixture, add vanilla pulp and vanilla perfume; to the other half, add cocoa powder and chocolate perfume. Cool slightly before filling into chocolate bar molds, then let cool completely. Let sit in molds for 2 to 3 days for cocoa butter to solidify, then unmold.

4 The bath bars can be kept for 6 to 12 months.

Tip: Bath bars will look best when packaged in cellophane wrap, but if you prefer, you may wrap them in aluminum foil instead.

Shower Jellies
(with Sodium Lauryl Sulfate)

For normal and oily skin

Ingredients

150 g (5.291 oz) SLS noodles *or* 60 g
   (2.116 oz) liquid SLS

Phase A

2.5 g (0.088 oz) carrageenan (kappa)

2.5 g (0.088 oz) table salt

0.3 g (0.011 oz) polyester glitter or mica

1 g (0.035 oz) guar gum

Phase B

170 g (5.996 oz) boiled tap water

10 g (0.353 oz) propylene glycol

130 g (4.585 oz) glycerin

1 g (0.035 oz) beet root extract (or other
   water-soluble colorant)

Phase C

60 g (2.116 oz) liquid surfactant

3.2 g (0.071 oz) Phenonip (liquid parabens)

8 g (0.282 oz) perfume oil or essential oils
   (4 drops mint and 4 drops lemon)

1 First, prepare a liquid surfactant if using
SLS noodles: Place 150 g (5.291 oz) SLS
noodles and 300 g (10.582 oz) tap water into
a beaker and bring to a boil while stirring
gently until the SLS has completely dissolved.
Remove any foam with a skimming ladle. Let
the liquid cool. The resulting clear syrupy
liquid will serve as base for the shower jellies.

2 In a large beaker, combine carrageenan
with salt, polyester glitter, and guar gum. In
a second beaker, mix tap water with propylene glycol, glycerin, and beet root extract and
bring the mixture to a boil. Pour this into the
carrageen-salt-glitter mixture while stirring
with a wire whisk (photo 1). There should be
no lumps. Continue stirring with a glass
stirrer.

3 Stir 60 g (2.116 oz) liquid surfactant
(homemade as per step 1 or store-bought),
Phenonip, and perfume oil into the liquid
(photo 2), taking care to avoid foaming.
Quickly pour the mixture into molds and let
cool for approximately 1 hour (photo 3); then
the jellies can be unmolded.

4 Stored cool, these shower jellies will keep
for approximately 3 months.

**Tips: Shower jellies are great for child-
ren: They feel as smooth and wobbly as
jello, sparkle, smell good, and on top of
that, they clean! In the summer, shower
jellies can be placed in the freezer for a
while. Afterward, they will still be bouncy
and, at the same time, plesantly cool and
refreshing.**

**This first recipe for shower jellies
with SLS (sodium lauryl sulfate) will
take slightly longer to prepare than the
second one for shower jellies without
SLS. Although SLS has been a traditional
ingredient in toothpastes, shampoos, and
shower gels, it is controversial. I seldom
use it; however, in a number of recipes—
as this one here—it produces better results. If you prefer not to use SLS, replace
it with SLSA (sodium lauryl sulfoacetate),
a powdered surfactant approved for use in
natural cosmetics, as given in the follow-
ing alternate recipe for shower jellies.**

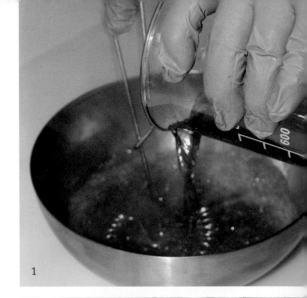

Shower Jellies
(with Sodium Lauryl Sulfoacetate)

For normal and oily skin

Ingredients

Phase A

2 g (0.071 oz) carrageenan (kappa)

0.5 g (0.018 oz) guar gum

2.6 g (0.212 oz) table salt

0.1 g (0.003 oz) grape extract (or other water-soluble colorant)

0.5 g (0.018 oz) polyester glitter or mica

10 g (0.353 oz) surfactant powder [sodium lauryl sulfoacetate (SLSA) or disodium lauryl sulfosuccinate]

Phase B

300 g (10.582 oz) tap water

100 g (3.527 oz) glycerin

Phase C

8 g (0.282 oz) perfume oil (5 drops orange and 3 drops cedarwood)

2 g (0.071 oz) Phenonip (liquid parabens)

1 Mix all Phase A ingredients in a large beaker. In a second beaker, bring to a boil tap water and glycerin. Combine perfume oil and Phenonip in a third beaker.

2 Add the boiling tap water with glycerin to Phase A and stir well using a wire whisk. Remove any foam before adding the perfume oil and the Phenonip. Pour the liquid into molds and keep in a cool place for approximately 1.5 hours.

Red Rose Peeling Oil

For dry, flaky skin

Ingredients

15 g (0.529 oz) coconut oil

2 g (0.071 oz) jojoba wax

2 g (0.071 oz) Ceralan™

25.5 g (0.899 oz) MCT oil (neutral oil)

20 g (0.705 oz) virgin soy oil

10 g (0.353 oz) virgin sunflower oil

8 g (0.282 oz) lysolecithin (or laureth-4)

5 g (0.176 oz) vitamin E acetate

7 g (0.247 oz) red jojoba beads

1.2 g (0.042 oz) silica

0.3 g (0.011 oz) tea rose perfume oil

1 Combine coconut oil, jojoba wax, and Ceralan™ in a beaker and melt on low heat. Switch off burner and add the remaining oils, stirring well. Let the mixture cool completely. Stir in lysolecithin (or laureth-4), vitamin E acetate, and jojoba beads.

2 When all ingredients have been thoroughly mixed, add silica and stir until it has completely dissolved. Finally, add perfume oil to the mixture. Because this peeling oil does not contain any water, no additional preservatives need to be added.

Tip: You may add 2 g (0.071 oz) sea-buckthorn berry oil and use white jojoba beads instead of the red ones. Sea-buckthorn berry oil goes well with orange essential oil.

Strawberry Shower Gel with Glitter

For all skin types

Ingredients

Phase A

90 g (3.175 oz) water

10 g (0.353 oz) glycerin

5 g (0.176 oz) D-panthenol

2 g (0.071 oz) silk protein

1 g (0.035 oz) beet root extract (or 1 pinch water-soluble pink-colored pigment)

20 g (0.705 oz) ethanol

1.5 g (0.053 oz) xanthan gum

Phase B

39 g (1.375 oz) coco-betaine

20 g (0.705 oz) surfactant blend

6 g (0.212 oz) almond oil

Phase C

4 g (0.141 oz) strawberry perfume oil

1 g (0.035 oz) polyester glitter

15 drops citric acid (for a pH of 5.5–6)

Optional: 20–40 drops Paraben K

1 Mix water, glycerin, D-panthenol, silk protein, and beet root extract in a beaker (photo 1).

2 Place ethanol into a second beaker, then stir in xanthan. While stirring continuously, pour the water with the other ingredients into the ethanol/xanthan mixture to create a gel (photo 2).

3 In a third beaker, mix coco-betaine, the surfactant blend, and almond oil. Pour this mixture carefully into the gel and mix thoroughly using an immersion blender (photo 3). Add perfume oil and polyester glitter. Finally, stir in citric acid. For preservation, add Paraben K.

4 Alcohol will preserve the shower gel for 8 to 12 weeks. If 40 drops Paraben K are used instead, the shower gel can be kept for 6 months.

Marzipan-Almond Washing Lotion

For sensitive, dry skin

Ingredients

25 g (0.882 oz) Facetensid HT

5 g (0.176 oz) coco-betaine

2.5 g (0.088 oz) sucrose cocoate

2.5 g (0.088 oz) fluid lecithin CM

2.5 g (0.088 oz) prune kernel oil

75 g (2.645 oz) almond milk

10 g (0.353 oz) Rewoderm®

2 drops bitter almond oil (hydrocyanic acid free)

1 g (0.035 oz) Phenonip

1 In a beaker, mix Facetensid HT, coco-betaine, sucrose cocoate, fluid lecithin CM, and prune kernel oil. Slowly pour this mixture into the almond milk while continuously stirring with a spatula until homogenous.

2 Add Rewoderm® to thicken your washing lotion. Depending on the desired consistency, you may use less Rewoderm® than stated in the recipe. Add bitter almond oil and Phenonip. Fill the washing lotion into a pump dispenser or bottle.

3 Without any preservatives added, this washing lotion will keep for about 4 weeks. Preserving with 1 g (0.035 oz) Phenonip will increase its shelf life to 12 weeks.

Shower Smoothie

For normal skin

Ingredients

65 g (0.176 oz) soap (preferably handmade and fragrance-free)

15 g (0.529 oz) neroli hydrolate

8 g (0.282 oz) glycerin

0.1 g (0.003 oz) xanthan gum

15 g (0.529 oz) aloe vera juice

2.5 g (0.088 oz) silk protein

2.5 g (0.088 oz) D-panthenol

1 g (0.035 oz) Optiphen

2.5 g (0.088 oz) honey

5 g (0.176 oz) shea butter

5 g (0.176 oz) jojoba oil

0.4 g (0.014 oz) sea-buckthorn berry oil

2 g (0.071 oz) essential oils [1 g (0.035 oz) ylang ylang, 1 g (0.035 oz) orange]

1   Finely grate the soap using a grater, then place the flakes in a beaker. In a second beaker, bring neroli hydrolate to a boil. Pour the neroli hydrolate over the soap flakes and allow to soak.

2   Meanwhile, put glycerin in another beaker and add xanthan while stirring.

3   To the beaker in which the neroli hydrolate was heated, add aloe vera juice, silk protein, D-panthenol, Optiphen, and honey. Stir until honey has completely dissolved. For this, briefly place beaker onto still warm burner if needed. To prevent degradation of valuable active ingredients, the liquid should not be heated to more than 75°C (167°F).

4   To create a gel, add glycerin/xanthan mixture under constant stirring. Add the resulting gel to the presoaked soap flakes.

5   Melt shea butter and add jojoba oil. Set this oil aside for the time being.

6   Using a handheld mixer, stand mixer, or immersion blender on high, blend the soap flake mixture until a homogeneous mass has formed. Then gradually stir in the oil. Continue stirring for another 2 to 3 minutes until the mass has approximately doubled in volume. The result should have the consistency of whipped cream.

7   Finally, add sea-buckthorn berry oil and essential oils, then pour the mixture into a decorative jar or container.

Tip: **Turn this shower smoothie into an exfoliant by mixing in a small amount of sugar, almond bran, stearic acid, or jojoba beads. The mass will separate if salt is added.**

Tea Tree Shampoo

Anti-dandruff

Ingredients

Phase A

40 g (1.411 oz) Plantapon® SF

6 g (0.212 oz) Lamesoft®

0.5 g (0.018 oz) neem oil

0.5 g (0.018 oz) broccoli seed oil

Phase B

20 g (0.705 oz) tea tree hydrolate

20 g (0.705 oz) rosemary hydrolate

Phase C

5 g (0.176 oz) nettle extract

2.5 g (0.088 oz) salvia extract

2.5 g (0.088 oz) neem extract

0.1 g (0.003 oz) xanthan gum

1 g (0.035 oz) piroctone olamine

2 g (0.071 oz) tea tree fluid

0.5 g (0.018 oz) Optiphen

1 g (0.035 oz) tea tree essential oil

0.4 g (0.014 oz) rosemary essential oil

0.3 g (0.011 oz) saline essential oil

1 drop green food coloring

lactic acid (80%) or citric acid (for a pH of 5.5–7)

1 Combine all phase A ingredients in a beaker.

2 Put nettle extract, salvia extract, and neem extract into a beaker and stir in xanthan. While stirring, add tea tree hydrolate and rosemary hydrolate until the consistency has become gel-like.

3 To the created gel, gradually add piroctone olamine, tea tree fluid, and Optiphen. Carefully pour Phase A into this mixture and stir everything well with a spatula, taking care not to create any foam. Now, add the essential oils and the food coloring.

4 Check the pH and add lactic or citric acid drop by drop, until the pH is at 5.5 to 7.

Rose & Vanilla Two-Phase Bathing Oil

For mature skin

Phase A

30 g (1.06 oz) Plantapon® SF

30 g (1.06 oz) rose water

7.5 g (0.264 oz) glycerin

1 g (0.035 oz) Optiphen

1 g (0.035 oz) Perlatin

1 pinch red rose pigment

Phase B

22 g (0.776 oz) jojoba oil

34.4 g (1.213 oz) almond oil

12 g (0.423 oz) evening primrose oil

11 g (0.388 oz) rosehip kernel oil

0.1 g (0.003 oz) rosehip kernel CO_2 extract

0.5 g (0.018 oz) rose perfume oil

0.5 g (0.018 oz) vanilla perfume oil

1 Mix all Phase A ingredients in one beaker and all Phase B ingredients in a second beaker.

2 Pour Phase A into a 150 ml (5 fl oz) bottle. Now, fill it up with Phase B.

3 Shake the bathing oil bottle before use to mix both phases.

Cleopatra's Secret

For dry, damaged hair

Ingredients

Phase A (water phase)

50 g (1.764 oz) distilled water

2 g (0.071 oz) Montanov™ S

Phase B

45 g (0.176 oz) Facetensid HT

2 g (0.071 oz) Perlatin

3 g (0.106 oz) broccoli seed oil

2 g (0.071 oz) fluid lecithin CM

Phase C

18 g (0.282 oz) donkey milk powder

7 g (0.247 oz) D-panthenol

10 g (0.353 oz) honey

0.5 g (0.018 oz) wheat protein (elastin)

13.5 g (0.476 oz) Rewoderm®

1 g (0.035 oz) vanilla perfume oil

1 g (0.035 oz) honey perfume oil

1 g (0.035 oz) Phenonip

Lactic acid (for a pH of 5.5–7)

1 In a beaker, bring distilled water to a boil and dissolve the Montanov™ S in it. While the water is cooling, mix Phase B ingredients with each other (photo 1).

2 When the water has cooled to 35°C (95°F), add the milk powder and briefly combine using a wire whisk or an immersion blender. Add in D-panthenol, honey, and wheat protein and stir until the honey has completely dissolved.

3 Pour Phase B into the water phase and carefully mix everything with a spatula, taking care to avoid foaming (photo 2). Thicken the shampoo with Rewoderm® until it has reached the desired consistency, keeping in mind that Rewoderm® will continue to thicken for some time.

4 Mix perfume oils and Phenonip into the shampoo (photo 3). Check the pH and add lactic acid drop by drop until pH is at 5.5 to 7.

Tip: If you've accidentally added too much Rewoderm®, simply dilute the shampoo with a small amount of water.

Body Care Products

This chapter is all about head-to-toe care for every skin type. Notes about the fat content of the various creams will give you an indication of what will be suitable for your skin type—the more mature and less moist your skin is, the more it has to be protected by added oils to prevent its further drying out. When making your choice, allow yourself to be tempted by such promising ingredients as coconut cream and mango butter, pineapple, lily of the valley, and frangipani perfume oils, or lemon, rose, or frankincense hydrolates. Besides body lotion and body butter preparations, you will find refreshing sun spray for particularly hot days, moisturizing after-sun gel, pick-me-up body splash that will shake you awake without fail every time, as well as a pleasantly fragrant jasmine-sandalwood body powder for the special moments in your life.

Hydro-Lipid Shake Lotion for Oily, Blemished Skin

Ingredients

Phase A (water phase)

18 g (0.282 oz) tea tree hydrolate

17.5 g (0.264 oz) lemon hydrolate

1.4 g (0.049 oz) glycerin

2 g (0.071 oz) silk protein

4 g (0.141 oz) urea

0.25 g (0.009 oz) sodium lactate

0.25 g (0.009 oz) lactic acid (approximately 6 drops)

0.1 g (0.003 oz) hyaluronic acid

6.5 g (0.229 oz) ethanol (95 vol%)

If needed, vegetable-based green or yellow colorant

Phase B (lipid phase)

6 g (0.212 oz) babassu oil

10 g (0.353 oz) safflower oil

8 g (0.282 oz) grape seed oil

6.6 g (0.233 oz) hemp oil

5 g (0.176 oz) MCT oil (neutral oil)

3 g (0.106 oz) evening primrose oil

10 g (0.353 oz) squalane

0.5 g (0.018 oz) vitamin E

0.5 g (0.018 oz) vitamin E acetate

0.4 g (0.014 oz) essential oils (4 drops tea tree, 3 drops manuka, 2 drops cajeput, 3 drops cedarwood)

1 Pour the tea tree hydrolate and the lemon hydrolate into a small beaker [8 to 10 ml (0.270 to 0.338 fl oz)]. Stir glycerin and silk protein into the hydrolates.

2 Add urea and mix until it has dissolved. Urea will dissolve only slowly in cold liquid. If needed, pulverize it in a small mortar prior to use to speed up the process. Also stir in sodium lactate and lactic acid until everything has dissolved.

3 In a second beaker, mix hyaluronic acid and ethanol for approximately 1 minute with an electric milk frother or other handheld mixer. Add the result to the hydrolate mixture while stirring, until a gel-like consistency has been reached. For visual contrast in the bottle, color the two phases using plant-based green or yellow dye, if you wish.

4 Melt the babassu oil in a beaker until clear. One after another, add the different oils, the squalane, vitamin E, vitamin E acetate, and essential oils.

5 Carefully pour first the water phase, then the lipid phase, into the bottle, one after the other. Shake the bottle before using to combine both phases.

6 Stored cool and dry, the prepared shake lotion will keep for approximately 4 to 6 weeks. It can be additionally preserved with potassium sorbate solution.

Tip: The lotion should have a pH of 5 to 5.5. When additionally preserved with potassium sorbate solution, the preservative should be added first before adjusting the pH with lactic acid. A pH of approximately 6.2 is regarded as ideal for urea.

Piña Colada Body Butter

For normal and dry skin

Ingredients

Phase A (lipid phase)

7 g (0.247 oz) emulsan

1.5 g (0.053 oz) candelilla wax

35 g (1.234 oz) virgin coconut oil (scented)

14 g (0.494 oz) shea butter

Phase B (water phase)

73.5 g (2.593 oz) coconut cream or distilled water

5 g (0.176 oz) glycerin

Phase C

2 g (0.071 oz) D-panthenol

1 g (0.035 oz) Phenonip [only 0.5 g (0.018 oz) when using water instead of coconut cream]

1 g (0.035 oz) pineapple (or piña colada) perfume oil

1 In a beaker, melt the emulgator (emulsan), the candelilla wax, and the coconut oil and heat the mixture to 75°C (167°F). Switch off the burner and add shea butter in small flakes. In a second beaker, bring the coconut cream (or water) and the glycerin to a boil and let the mixture cool to 70°C (158°F). When the shea butter has melted, both phases should have a temperature of 70°C (158°F).

2 Pour the water phase (coconut cream and glycerine) into the lipid phase in small increments and mix with an immersion blender on high speed for 2 to 3 minutes, until a stable emulsion has formed. Now, continue stirring with a glass stirrer until the emulsion has cooled to about 35°C (95°F). Add the D-panthenol, Phenonip, and perfume oil and mix everything well.

3 The body butter will keep for approximately 4 weeks.

Tip: The amount of preservative used may look high, but it is necessary because of the fresh ingredient coconut cream. When preparing the body with water instead of coconut cream, 0.5 g (0.018 oz) Phenonip is sufficient.

Mango-Apricot Lotion (20% fat)

For normal skin

Ingredients

Phase A (lipid phase)

5 g (0.176 oz) apricot oil

3 g (0.106 oz) camellia seed oil

2 g (0.071 oz) MCT oil (neutral oil)

1 g (0.035 oz) cetyl alcohol

4.5 g (0.159 oz) glyceryl stearate SE

3 g (0.106 oz) mango butter

Phase B (water phase)

48 g (0.282 oz) neroli hydrolate

Phase C

12 g (0.423 oz) ethanol (95 vol%)

0.4 g (0.014 oz) xanthan gum

10 g (0.353 oz) neroli hydrolate

1 g (0.035 oz) glycerin

2 g (0.071 oz) algae gel

2 g (0.071 oz) cucumber extract

Phase D

20 drops Paraben K

Optional: 1 drop lactic acid, 80%

10 drops apricot flavoring

10 drops mango flavoring

1 Place all of the Phase A ingredients, except for the mango butter, into a beaker and heat to 65°C (149°F) in a water bath. Using a second beaker, heat Phase B ingredient separately in a water bath to 65°C (149°F) too.

2 Meanwhile, stir the xanthan into the ethanol. In yet another beaker, combine the remaining Phase C ingredients, then stir this mix into the ethanol/xanthan mixture until a gel has formed.

3 When the oil and water phases have reached 65°C (149°F), add the mango butter to the lipid phase and stir until it has melted.

4 Stir the water phase into the lipid phase for up to 1 minute on high, until a stable emulsion has formed, then continue stirring with a glass stirrer or spatula. When the emulsion has cooled to 30 to 35°C (86° to 95°F), add it to Phase C while constantly stirring and mix everything. Add the fragrances at the very end.

5 If preserving additionally with Paraben K, test the pH now. If it's more than 8, carefully add 1 drop of lactic acid. Paraben K is only able to preserve at pHs up to 8. Please note: Even a single drop of lactic acid can cause the phases to separate. To be on the safe side, dilute the lactic acid with a small amount of distilled or boiled water (5:1).

6 Finally, pour your Mango-Apricot Lotion into a pump dispenser. When preserved with 12% alcohol, the lotion will keep for 10 to 12 weeks. Paraben K will prolong its shelf life even further.

Tip: I've opted for food flavorings because their mango and apricot scents have a more genuine aroma than perfume oil. Here, I've use the same flavorings as for lip balms and glosses.

Note: The emulgator glyceryl stearate SE is not as easy to work with as the emulgator emulsan—emulsions may turn unstable and phases separate. When glyceryl stearate SE is present, the temperatures of the oil and water phases should never exceed 65°C (149°F). It also reacts sensitively to acids and mineral salts. The ideal pH for glyceryl stearate is at 6.8 to 8.2 (slightly alkaline). For this reason, don't use potassium sorbate solution or other preservatives needing a slightly acidic pH. Lastly, glyceryl stearate may not be agitated vigorously. Instead of an immersion blender, use a milk frother, and only briefly stir on high speed. As soon as the phases have combined, continue stirring with a glass stirrer or spatula. The emulsion will thicken during cooling.

Raspberry-Currant Body Lotion (25% fat)

For dry skin

Ingredients

Phase A (water phase)

55 g (1.940 oz) currant hydrolate

1 pinch rose red pigment (or 1 drop beet root extract)

Phase B (lipid phase)

3 g (0.106 oz) emulsan

1.5 g (0.053 oz) ceto-stearyl alcohol

6 g (0.212 oz) almond oil

9 g (0.317 oz) babassu oil

3 g (0.106 oz) shea butter

Phase C

10 g (0.353 oz) currant hydrolate

1.5 g (0.053 oz) aloe vera powder, 10:1

0.5 g (0.018 oz) wheat protein (elastin)

5 g (0.176 oz) Natural Moisturizing Factor NMF

Phase D

2.5 g (0.088 oz) raspberry seed oil

1 g (0.035 oz) tocopherol

1 g (0.035 oz) vitamin E acetate

1–2 drops lactic acid, 80%

10 drops raspberry perfume oil

10–20 drops Paraben K (alternatively: 20 drops potassium sorbate solution, 5:1)

1 Heat Phase A ingredients in a water bath to 75°C (167°F). With the exception of shea butter, also heat Phase B ingredients in a water bath to 75°C (167°F) in a second beaker.

2 Meanwhile, place the currant hydrolate from Phase C in a small beaker and, while stirring with a milk frother, add first the aloe vera powder, then the wheat protein and the Natural Moisturizing Factor NMF.

3 As soon as the oil and water phases have reached the same temperature, switch off the burner and stir the shea butter into the lipid phase until it has completely melted.

4 Gradually stir the water phase into the lipid phase with an immersion blender on high speed for 2 to 3 minutes, until a stable emulsion has formed. Continue stirring with a spatula until the cream has cooled to 35°C (95°F). Now add, drop by drop and while constantly stirring, the raspberry seed oil, tocopherol, raspberry perfume oil, and vitamin E acetate.

5 Adjust the pH to 5.5 by adding 1 to 2 drops lactic acid. After this, preserve the body lotion with 10 drops Paraben K or 20 drops potassium sorbate solution. When preserving with potassium sorbate solution, stir the granules into Phase C before adding Phase C to the emulsion. Finally, pour the body lotion into a jar or bottle.

6 The body lotion will keep for 3 months; with the double amount Paraben K, for 6 months.

Body Butter with Argan & Pomegranate Oil (30% fat)

For dry, mature skin

Ingredients

Phase A (lipid phase)

8 g (0.282 oz) jojoba oil

6 g (0.212 oz) argan oil

3 g (0.106 oz) emulsan

3 g (0.106 oz) cetyl alcohol

6 g (0.212 oz) mango butter

Phase B (water phase)

53 g (1.870 oz) rose hydrolate

2.3 g (0.081 oz) glycerin

Phase C

5.2 g (0.183 oz) ethanol (95 vol%)

0.1 g (0.003 oz) xanthan gum

Phase D

4 g (0.141 oz) pomegranate kernel oil

5 g (0.176 oz) Natural Moisturizing Factor NMF

2 g (0.071 oz) D-panthenol

0.4 g (0.014 oz) collagen

1 g (0.035 oz, approximately 20 drops) potassium sorbate solution, 5:1 [equals 0.2 g (0.007 oz) potassium sorbate granules]

1 g (0.035 oz, approximately 20 drops) lily of the valley perfume oil

2 drops lactic acid, 80% (for a pH of 5.5)

1 Place all Phase A ingredients, except for the mango butter, in a beaker and heat to 75°C (167°F). In a second beaker, combine rose hydrolate and glycerin and heat both to 75°C (167°F) too.

2 Meanwhile, put the ethanol into a third beaker and dissolve the xanthan in it.

3 As soon as the correct temperature has been reached, turn off the burner. Leave the beakers in the water bath. Add the mango butter into the lipid phase and stir until it has completely melted.

4 Stir the ethanol/xanthan mixture into the water phase until it turns into a fluid gel.

5 Gradually, add the water phase into the lipid phase and stir both for 2 to 3 minutes with an immersion blender or milk frother on high until a stable emulsion has formed. Then, continue stirring with a spatula until the emulsion has cooled to about 35°C (95°F). One drop at a time, add first the pomegranate kernel oil, then the remaining Phase D ingredients. Finally, fill the body butter into a jar.

6 The body butter will keep for 3 months.

Hemp & Avocado Body Butter (40% fat)

For dry, flaky skin

Ingredients

Phase A (lipid phase)

1 g (0.035 oz) Avocadin®

15 g (0.529 oz) macadamia nut oil

5 g (0.176 oz) avocado oil

6 g (0.212 oz) glyceryl stearate

8 g (0.282 oz) shea butter

Phase B (water phase)

35 g (1.234 oz) frankincense hydrolate

Phase C

0.4 g (0.014 oz) allantoin

12 g (0.423 oz) frankincense hydrolate

2.5 g (0.088 oz) aloe vera powder, 10:1

Phase D

6 g (0.212 oz) ethanol

0.1 g (0.003 oz) xanthan gum

Phase E

5 g (0.176 oz) hemp oil

2 g (0.071 oz) tocopherol

1 g (0.035 oz, approximately 20 drops) potassium sorbate solution, 5:1

1 drop lactic acid if needed

1 Place all of the Phase A ingredients except shea butter into a beaker in a water bath and heat to 75°C (167°F). In a second beaker, heat 35 g (1.234 oz) frankincense hydrolate to 75°C (167°F) too.

2 Meanwhile, put the ethanol in a third beaker and dissolve the xanthan in it.

3 As soon as the lipid phase and the water phase have both reached a temperature of 75°C (167°F), turn off the burner. Add the shea butter into the lipid phase and stir until it has completely melted.

4 Add the allantoin to the remaining 12 g (0.423 oz) frankincense hydrolate and stir until it has dissolved. Stir in the aloe vera powder to create a gel.

5 Stir ethanol/xanthan mixture into the water phase until a gel-like consistency has been reached. Using an immersion blender on high for 2 to 3 minutes, blend the mixture gradually into the lipid phase until a stable emulsion has formed. Continue stirring with a spatula until the emulsion has cooled to 35°C (95°F).

6 Gradually, while continuing to stir, add Phase C into the emulsion. Finally, one drop at a time, add first the hemp oil, then the remaining Phase E ingredients. Test the pH, and, if needed, add a drop of lactic acid to adjust. Pour the body butter into a cosmetic jar.

Tip: If desired, the body butter can be enhanced with an added scent, although it smells pleasant enough even without additional fragrance. Apply this very rich body butter to your still-damp skin after a bath for nourishment.

Cooling Sun Spray

For dry skin

Ingredients

0.1 g (0.003 oz) hyaluronic acid

5 g (0.176 oz) ethanol (95 vol%)

4 g (0.141 oz) D-panthenol

5 g (0.176 oz) aloe vera, 10:1

5 g (0.176 oz) urea

4 drops squalane

80 g (2.82 fl oz) distilled water

Place all of the ingredients, except for the water, into a 100 ml (3.3 fl oz) spray bottle, then fill up with distilled and cooled water. Shake the bottle prior to use to combine the essential oils with the water.

Variations

For an increased cooling effect, you can dissolve a pinch of menthol crystals in warm water and add to the mixture, or replace the water with peppermint hydrolate.

Instead of ethanol, substitute plant extracts (such as extract of Asiatic penny-wort). Since these extracts very often contain only 70% alcohol, less water has to be used to fill up the bottle: With 70 vol% alcohol, use 1 g (0.035 oz) extract and 75 g (2.645 oz) water.

If you want this sun spray to double as a mosquito repellent, add 1 g (0.035 oz) each of tea tree oil and lavender oil.

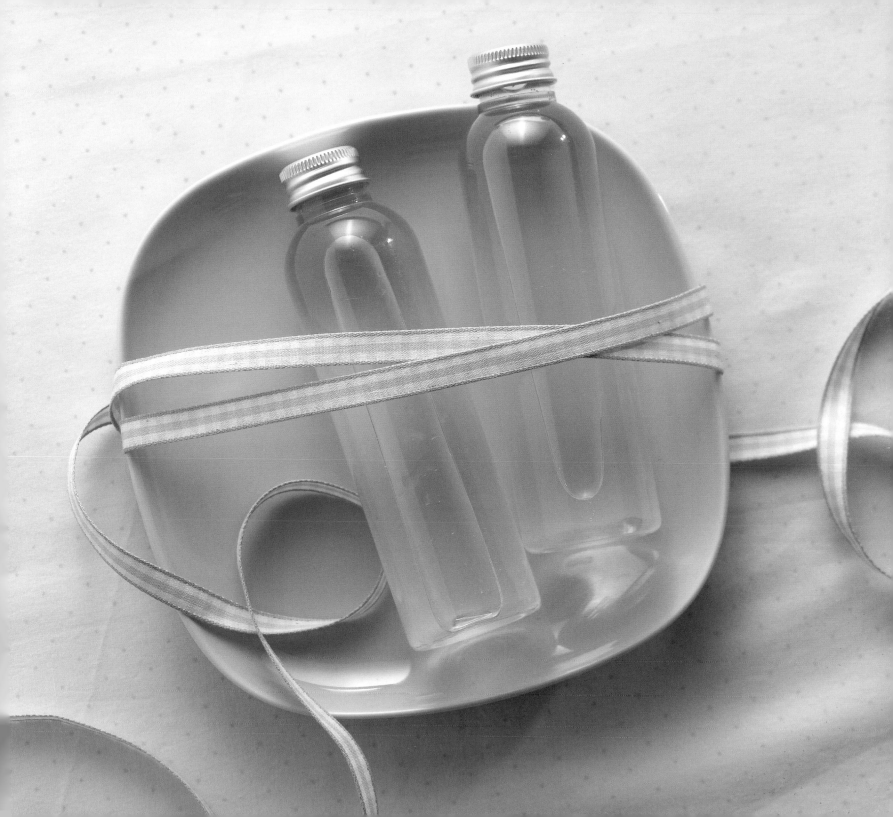

After-Sun Gel

Ingredients

Phase A

6 g (0.212 oz) ethanol

1.8 g (0.063 oz) xanthan gum

Phase B

0.5 g (0.018 oz) aloe vera powder, 200:1

0.1 g (0.003 oz) hyaluronic acid

3 g (0.106 oz) glycerin

34 g (0.141 oz) German chamomile hydrolate

Phase C

40 g (1.411 oz) lavender hydrolate

2 g (0.071 oz) D-panthenol

5 g (0.176 oz) urea

1 g (0.035 oz) sodium lactate

7 drops lactic acid, 80%

Optional: 0.1 g (0.003 oz) grape extract (colorant)

Phase D

6 g (0.212 oz) MCT oil (neutral Oil)

0.5 g (0.018 oz) Optiphen or 20 drops Paraben K

10 drops lavender essential oil

10 drops ylang ylang essential oil

Optional: 1 teaspoon Q10 beads

1 Place the ethanol in a large beaker and dissolve the xanthan in it.

2 In a second beaker, combine aloe vera powder and hyaluronic acid with glycerin and German chamomile hydrolate. Lumps, if any, will dissolve with time.

3 In a third beaker, mix Phase C ingredients until well dissolved. Now, using an immersion blender on high speed for approximately 30 seconds, stir Phase C ingredients into Phase A (photo 1). Continue stirring with a spatula until a gel-like consistency has been achieved (photo 2). Now add Phase B, and finally, one ingredient after another, all of the Phase D ingredients.

Tip: Q10 pearls are included because their golden color just looks good in this After-Sun Gel. However, Q10 reputedly also promotes cellular energy production, acts as a free radical fighter, and prevents premature aging of the skin. The grape extract (colorant), which by the way will not show on the skin, is also nonessential but pleasing to the eye.

Pick-Me-Up Body Splash

Ingredients

Phase A

70 g (2.469 oz) lemon hydrolate

3 g (0.106 oz) urea

2 g (0.071 oz) sodium lactate

0.3 g (0.011 oz, approximately 10 drops) lactic acid

4.5 g (0.159 oz) algae gel

5 g (0.176 oz) cucumber extract

2 g (0.071 oz) glycerin

Phase B

12 g (0.423 oz) ethanol

0.2 g (0.007 oz) hyaluronic acid

0.1 g (0.003 oz) xanthan gum

Phase C

20 drops Paraben K

2 drops lemon essential oil

2 drops pink grapefruit essential oil

2 drops lime essential oil

2 drops green tangerine essential oil

3 drops frangipani essential oil or frangipani perfume essential oil

1 First, combine all Phase A ingredients in a beaker. Place the ethanol in a large beaker [150 ml (5 fl oz)] and mix the hyaluronic acid and the xanthan into it. Now add Phase A to Phase B, while stirring with a spatula, until a low-viscosity gel has formed.

2 Finally, add Phase C ingredients. Decant the body splash into a spray bottle and store it in the refrigerator to enhance the stimulating effect of the formulation.

3 When stored cool, the body splash will keep for 3 months.

Tip: Frangipani essential oil is pricey. For a more economical replacement, try frangipani perfume oil instead. It smells just as nice, or even better.

Jasmine-Sandalwood Body Powder

Ingredients

Phase A

16 g (0.212 oz) kaolin (white lava clay)

10 g (0.353 oz) corn starch

6 g (0.212 oz) silk powder

3 g (0.106 oz) low-luster pigment

2 g (0.071 oz) magnesium stearate

1 g (0.035 oz) zinc oxide

Phase B

10 g (0.353 oz) cocoa butter

3 drops *Jasminum sambac* essential oil

5 drops sandalwood essential oil

1 Place all of the Phase A ingredients into a Ziploc® bag and knead the bag for a few minutes, until the contents has been thoroughly mixed.

2 Put the cocoa butter into a beaker and melt it in a water bath.

3 Evenly distribute 20 drops of the melted cocoa butter and the essential oils throughout the powder in the bag. Reclose the bag and knead the contents vigorously once more.

4 Place the powder into a mortar and thoroughly pulverize it by moving the pestle in a circular motion. Finally, passing the powder through a sieve, fill it into a compact to store.

About the Author

Jinaika Jakuszeit, mother of four, has been busy creating natural cosmetics for ten years now. With a solid basis as a registered German naturopath and a vast background knowledge on the subject, mostly obtained through teaching herself, she was brave and energetic enough to turn her hobby into a career. Her recipes have been developed and fine-tuned to perfection with lots of experience and attention to detail. In fact, the product descriptions for her cosmetic formulations almost read like poetry! Besides developing new ideas and recipes, she shares her experience and sparkling creativity by teaching classes, workshops, and training seminars.

Acknowledgments

I would like to take the opportunity to thank all those who have taught me much of what I know today. First of all, my friend Petra Neumann, from whom I have learned a lot about chemistry and cosmetics, and who has helped me to optimize a few of my recipes. With her originates the recipe for the Cooling Sun Spray on page 136. Furthermore, my colleague and role model Brigitte Bräutigam, whose books on cosmetics I have devoured. Without her, I'd probably not even know how to mix a cream today! Thank you to my friends Andrea Gerlach and Dorothee Matheuser, who have penned my author's biography, and on whose honest opinion I can always count.

I also would like to thank my parents, who always support me, and first and foremost, my husband and our four children, who test everything I concoct without complaints, and on whom I can always count, even if things get a bit stressful.

With any questions about my recipes, you may contact me any time through my blog at http://traumseifen.blogspot.com. I will be glad to help!

Resources

Some of the ingredients used in this book are proprietary brand-name blends, which may not be available from all sources (or in all countries). By referencing the INCI name(s) and properties of these ingredients, you should be able to find suitable replacements if needed. Listed below are several European and American sources for many of the skin care ingredients used in this book (for foreign sources, use Google Translate). There are many other sources also available, which may be easily found online.

Allerlei-Praktisches (Switzerland)
Cosmetic raw materials
www.allerlei-praktisches.ch

Aroma-Zone (France)
A variety of ingredients
www.aroma-zone.com

Art of Beauty (Austria)
Cosmetic raw materials
www.art-of-beauty.at

Bulk Actives (USA)
Ingredients for skin care
www.bulkactives.com

Essential Wholesale & Labs (USA)
A variety of ingredients and blending services
www.essentialwholesale.com

Lotion Crafter (USA)
Ingredients and equipment
www.lotioncrafter.com

Making Cosmetics (USA)
Great selection of cosmetic ingredients
www.makingcosmetics.com

Manske (Germany)
A variety of skin-care supplies
www.manske-shop.com

Sonnenelixier (Germany)
Essential and cold-pressed oils
www.sonnenelixier.de